I0049714

How to Develop Your Presentation Skills

Creating Success books are available at
www.koganpage.com/creating-success
and booksellers worldwide

THE **CREATING SUCCESS** SERIES
Over 1.8 million copies sold

How to Deal with Difficult People by Roy Lilley
How to Develop Your Presentation Skills by Theo Theobald
How to Improve Your Communication Skills by Alan Barker
How to Interpret Data by Nicholas Kelly
How to Manage People by Michael Armstrong
How to Manage Projects by Paul J Fielding
How to Manage Remotely by Gemma Dale
How to Mange Your Time Effectively by Patrick Forsyth
How to Negotiate by Mike Clayton
How to Organize Yourself by John Caunt
How to Write a Business Plan by Brian Finch
How to Write a Marketing Plan by John Westwood
How to Write Reports and Proposals by Patrick Forsyth

ABOUT THE AUTHOR

Theo Theobald has spent most of his adult life in front of an audience, as management trainer, stand-up comic and most recently funeral celebrant, writing and conducting countless services. A media career including a senior role with the BBC was followed by 20 years as a freelancer.

Sixth edition

How to Develop Your Presentation Skills

Inspire and inform with clarity and confidence

Theo Theobald

KoganPage

Publisher's note
Every possible effort has been made to ensure that the information contained in this book is accurate at the time of going to press, and the publishers and authors cannot accept responsibility for any errors or omissions, however caused. No responsibility for loss or damage occasioned to any person acting, or refraining from action, as a result of the material in this publication can be accepted by the editor, the publisher or the author.

First published in Great Britain and the United States in 2011 by Kogan Page Limited
Sixth edition 2026

All rights reserved. No part of this publication may be reproduced, stored or transmitted by any means without prior written permission from Kogan Page, except as permitted under applicable copyright laws.

Kogan Page
Kogan Page Ltd, 2nd Floor, 45 Gee Street, London EC1V 3RS, United Kingdom
Kogan Page Inc, 8 W 38th Street, Suite 902, New York, NY 10018, USA
www.koganpage.com

EU Representative (GPSR)
Authorised Rep Compliance Ltd, Ground Floor, 71 Baggot Street Lower, Dublin D02 P593, Ireland
www.arccompliance.com

Kogan Page books are printed on paper from sustainable forests.

© Theo Theobald, 2011, 2013, 2016, 2019, 2022, 2026

The moral rights of the author have been asserted in accordance with the Copyright, Designs and Patents Act 1988.

ISBNs
Hardback   978 1 3986 2262 3
Paperback   978 1 3986 2261 6
Ebook   978 1 3986 2263 0

British Library Cataloguing-in-Publication Data
A CIP record for this book is available from the British Library.

Library of Congress Cataloging-in-Publication Data
2025038029

Typeset by Hong Kong FIVE Workshop, Hong Kong
Printed and bound by CPI Group (UK) Ltd, Croydon CR0 4YY

For Nancy

CONTENTS

PREFACE

As the world of communication evolves and changes at an ever-increasing pace, it's sometimes wise to pause, catch your breath and really think about how and where you fit in. Are you really making the impact you'd like?

Whatever new channels come on stream, to deliver more and more content, the things that cut through like nothing else, are both what you say *and* how you say it.

Being a great presenter will get you noticed.

Proof of the importance of this skill is right here in your hands; as the sixth edition of this book is published, the longevity of the subject matter is self-evident. But since its first publication back in 2011 the text has gone through its own evolution, responding to the needs of business and beyond, delivering up-to-date advice on an age-old topic.

What this means in practical terms is that the core skills, the foundation stones of great public speaking, are all covered in detail, with practical advice and guidance on what to try, when and how. But these techniques are useless if they're not set against the changing landscape of the real world – falling attention spans, ever more communication 'noise', less face-to-face contact as remote working takes hold, the boundless influence of AI.

The challenge of getting your voice heard under *these* conditions is greater than ever, but with study of the text and by following the suggested activities, you will see a real and measurable improvement in your presentation performance.

Where that leads is up to you, but how you appear to others, with increased confidence, assertiveness and purpose, is bound to make a positive impact on your working life and social time.

Practice makes perfect, so a lot of your learning will be 'experiential'. It will be based upon the time you spend presenting; the more 'flying hours' you clock up, the better.

This sixth edition of *How to Develop Your Presentation Skills* is designed to supplement that to give you the best chance of writing and 'performing' to the very best of your ability.

As with the last edition, my parting shot before letting you launch yourself into the book is to remind you that you are unique and it is your take on the subject in hand that the audience wants to hear.

The most important thing of all, is *be yourself*.

Introduction

There are dozens of books you could have chosen to improve your presentation skills, but this is the right one. So, there you have it – the first, and most important, rule of becoming a consummate presenter: confidence. Or, and this is the really critical bit, the *appearance* of confidence. No one need ever know if you are shaking inside, if you are terrified of your audience or mortified at the thought of making a gaffe; as long as you appear to be in control you will always look professional.

I hope that by following some of the advice here, which is based on long personal experience, both good and bad, and many, many conversations with business speakers and professionals from the stage, you give yourself the chance to be the best you possibly can.

Powerful presentations are a matter of two things, internal and external factors; the first is all about you, the unique package of personality, experience, upbringing and environment that sets you apart from every other being on the planet.

Beyond that, there are the 'external factors'. I would define these as the nuts and bolts of presenting; the things you can learn, practise and master. They include everything from writing and rehearsing your script, through to ensuring that you are introduced properly, weighing up the dynamics of the room and relying on the tools of the trade, from microphones to visual aids.

Combining the two sets of parameters will help you achieve your 'personal best': a presentation that people will be talking about for a long time afterwards, for all the right reasons!

Before you jump in and start trying out new techniques, I hope that a bit of my own personal experience might help you. Right from the early days of doing presentations, I always wanted to be good at it, so I read many books, watched great speakers, noted what they did well and tried to incorporate it into my 'act'. I also listened to mentors, who would gladly offer advice on the best way to improve.

The downside of this is that I would stand up to speak with far too many thoughts running through my head: don't forget to smile, watch your body language, stop moving around the stage, slow your pace down, allow a bit of rise and fall in your voice and on and on. The truth is, I was so nervous that it was impossible to think of all these things at once.

So, what I would say to you, if you are still on an upward learning curve of speech making, is just concentrate on getting through it. Ensure that you know the content of your presentation as well as you can and use your instincts to deliver it in the best way you think fit. The more practice you get, the more able you will be to start thinking about some of the more advanced techniques. For now, congratulate yourself on having had the skill and resilience to get up and speak in public.

Let's be honest, you can't throw a stick these days without hitting a podcast and once you have, it's pretty much guaranteed that minutes after you begin to listen, there will be mention made of artificial intelligence; as buzzwords go, they don't buzz any louder.

When I wrote the first edition of this book, it was to replace an existing one that my publisher had commissioned some years earlier about the same topic. Some of the advice contained within the original's pages included a plea to always keep your acetates clean, so that they'd be in tip top condition when you put them on the overhead projector. You may well be wondering 'what's he on about?' I'm just trying to illustrate how quickly technology has changed.

Up to now, that's been largely to do with hardware or software, but AI is different. It 'thinks'; but more than this, it 'learns'. It's an evolving technology, driven by vast quantities of data and in the time it takes to read this book, AI will have learned some more.

For a while, I wanted to believe I was better than it, especially in creative terms, that my collection of experiences and the firing of random synapses in my brain couldn't be matched by a machine.

This far down the line, I'm forced to admit I was wrong and that in some aspects of presentation skills, AI beats me hands down.

Fortunately, for now, it's only some aspects.

If you've not engaged with AI yet, you should. What you'll quickly find out is that the more you feed it, the better it gets. Ask for a 20-minute presentation on the benefits of performance management and it'll give you the wisdom of countless managers who have presented similar content before. Tell it how you want it to sound, give it some context (size of your company, the audience you're talking to, where you're based, what you do) and it'll find a more relevant voice. Keep feeding it and you'll be able to get it to sound like you.

Most people I speak to about AI today agree with me as far as the current state of the art; fabulous for the grunt work, it saves you so much time doing the boring stuff, but only really useful when you add your own input, inject the individual personality that is you. My cast iron, nailed on advice for any elevator pitch on public speaking or presenting is 'be yourself'. At the moment AI can't do that with the same authenticity that you can.

I'm sure you're aware of the occasions when actors fall out with directors or writers. When they've played the same character for a while, they might say 'I don't think he/she would say that'. It's a bit the same with AI; you will know best whether or not the words it's feeding you would sound right coming out of your mouth.

You have the human ability to think on your feet, instantaneously, in real time, so, in the moment, during a presentation, you can add to the audience's experience by how you react to an occurrence, or the way you deliver a line; it is the quickness of your wits which outpaces the large language model.

This may not always be the case, and down the line, we might find it harder and harder to compete with the content provision and the method of delivery. But all of that is for a different book I think. If, in terms of presentation skills, you feel the need to get one up on AI, remember that you have the ability to smile!

The chapters that follow are in rough chronological order, inasmuch as you have to write your presentation before you rehearse. In order to consolidate the learning of each chapter, there is a short, optional activity at the end for you to try out, along with a summary, in bullet point form, of what you have just read. If there is a particular area of expertise that you are trying to master, it might be worth revisiting the relevant chapter summaries when you are next in the process of preparing to speak.

If you are still not sure of where to start with brushing up on your skills, use the sorting grid opposite (Figure 0.1) to decide on your priorities. Consider all the elements of making speeches, including:

- presentation skills;
- writing;
- rehearsal;
- use of voice;
- appearance of confidence;
- visual aids;
- assembling the right kit;
- finding low-risk opportunities to practise;
- humour;
- storytelling;
- handling nerves;
- handling an audience.

Figure 0.1   Sorting grid for presentation skills

Degree of impact

	High	**Low**
Easy	**Top priority** These are the actions that are easy to accomplish and have a big impact, e.g. buy a smart new suit!	**Secondary** Easy to do, but with not so much impact, e.g. pulling together a kit of parts, laptop, projector, marker pens, etc.
Hard	**Future planning** Difficult to achieve, but worth it in the end, e.g. become an excellent exponent of autocue.	**Forget it!** Not worth the effort and it would have little impact anyway.

Level of difficulty

01
What's your motivation?

In this chapter, we will look at the reasons why you want to improve your presentation skills, before taking time to think about who you are. What personal attributes do you already possess that will make you an even better presenter?

Very often we launch off on developing a new skill with only a vague reason why. It might be that you are increasingly called upon to stand up and deliver in front of an audience because of your job role, or perhaps you have seen and admired presentations given by a professional at work and that has made you aspire to be better.

If reinforcement of your decision were needed, below is a list of really good reasons to be a great presenter:

- Working life is competitive and if you are going to succeed you will need to develop the skills of influencing and persuasion, so that your ideas get heard and adopted. The best way to do this is face to face and presentations allow you the opportunity to 'persuade' a large group all at once.

- The confidence gained from being a good public speaker can be translated into other areas of your business or personal life. Acquiring the skills of building effective arguments and delivering them well is likely to come in handy, even in small meetings, where you will be perceived as articulate and professional.

- Presenting well is enjoyable. It is one thing to have good ideas and innovative solutions, but the ability to convey these to a wider audience is a much more difficult skill set. When you manage to do it well, there is a great feeling of satisfaction.

- Good presenters are often seen as having more authority than their peers. Being asked by the MD to speak at the next conference will do your profile and career prospects no end of good.

- 'Entertainers' tend to be well liked. I am not advocating that this is the start of your stage career, but employing the right set of 'stage skills' will help to win you friends in business and beyond.

- The best ideas can get left on the shelf. If we don't have the gift of being able to present effectively, our frustrations may grow as our voice gets lost in the wilderness. It is one thing to develop a killer strategy, another entirely to get it adopted.

- Risk is a part of what all of us do and there can often be a direct correlation with reward. Presenting to an audience allows us the opportunity to take risks on our own terms and it is something we can build on, as our confidence grows.

- The skill of being a great presenter will always look good on your CV/résumé. The same attributes will also help you outline your ideas and enthusiasm at a job interview. In fact there is a section on how to do this later in the book.

- Challenge and resilience are a necessary part of achieving your goals, so overcoming nerves and speaking with confidence in public will give you practice of core skills.

- Planning and preparation, so necessary for effective manage-ment, are the most important parts of an excellent presentation; they will provide another string to your bow.

So, there are many benefits, both business and social, to being 'good on your feet'. Getting that way is not as difficult as you might think.

Personal goal setting

Having decided that you want to improve your speaking technique, it is time to be honest and think about how much. The list of great modern orators includes Bill Clinton, Martin Luther King, Nelson Mandela and Barack Obama – all leaders of one sort or another on the world stage.

We can learn a lot from studying these people and the techniques they use, but we cannot *be* them, we can only be ourselves. And here is the most important point of this whole book; the title has been carefully chosen as *Develop Your Presentation Skills*. It is about maximizing *your* personal potential, making you the best you can possibly be. So set your expectations realistically; don't try to *become* the people you admire, just learn from them and adapt your new knowledge to enhance your own presentation persona.

The presenter's alter ego

Up there on stage, many of the best presenters appear to be 'larger than life'. If you meet them afterwards, they are most likely very much the same as the person you have just witnessed, but then they return to their 'normal' selves again. One of the reasons for this is that they are 'putting on a performance' when they present. Their gestures appear bigger and their passion greater because they have recognized that in order to get their message across effectively, they need to exaggerate themselves a little.

I am not suggesting that it is a conscious process, but it seems as if they have created an alter ego, literally an alternative version of themselves, who gets up and does the hard work on their behalf. This can be a very helpful technique when attempting to overcome nerves and deliver a big presentation. In a sense, it is the more confident, outgoing, risk-taking side of our character that comes to the fore.

Good idea

All of us are familiar with the skill of adapting to our circumstances; we show alternative sides of our character depending on who we are with. The version of you who gets up to speak needs to be the most professional, confident, outgoing one you can muster. I once asked an excellent presenter how she conquered her nerves and she replied: 'I just put the actress up there.'

The tools and techniques your alternative self will use are explained as we go through the chapters, but these are only of any use when allied to you, the speaker.

Who are you?

No, really, it's a serious question. What do people see when they meet you?

An entire industry has grown up in recent years around the topic of emotional intelligence (the softer 'people' skills) that great leaders use, as a matter of course. One of the foundation stones of these principles is that of self-awareness and it is really important when you are making a speech.

Perhaps you have been in a situation at some point in your life when someone has told you about a perception that has taken you by surprise. Maybe a good friend has said 'When I first met you, I thought you were a bit stand-offish.' This could, for example, have been a simple misinterpretation of your 'shyness' on that person's part. Whatever the cause, the outcome is the same.

The big question is: 'Can we influence the way we are perceived by an audience, when we stand up to speak?' The answer is only a 'yes' if we take the time in advance to think about the main factors that might affect this. Being realistic about where we are now and setting some improvement targets helps our self-awareness, which ultimately should improve our overall performance.

All of these topics are covered in much greater detail shortly, but for now, consider some of the things which make for great presentations and truly memorable speakers.

Where's the 'wow' factor?

Passion

We are all passionate about something. Each one of us has pet subjects that we get fired up about; big things, like politics and religion, or the trivial 'stuff of life' that can drive us mad. D H Lawrence once said, 'Be still when you have nothing to say; when genuine passion moves you, say what you've got to say, and say it hot.'

Audiences like to see passion from their host. It is an admirable quality when harnessed in the right direction, so showing a will to win, a desire to overcome injustice or a longing simply to make things better will always score great points for you. Passion is hard to practise and even harder to fake, but if you write material that you feel passionate about, your feelings will follow when you are presenting.

Wit

Are you quick-witted – either in the sense that you can instantly spot the funny side of a situation, or that you are bright, have your 'wits' about you? Both of these definitions are useful assets in the presentation arena. Even when you are meticulously prepared, things can, and often do, go wrong.

If you are able to show the members of an audience that you are unfazed by such events, you will win their hearts. A speaker who can rescue the situation when the PowerPoint fails, rather than stomping off the stage in a hissy fit, will definitely make friends and influence people.

Equally, if you are able to crack a joke in response to something that has just happened in the room, you will also endear yourself. This can be especially true if you have a question and answer session at the end of your address.

Professionalism

This is a word that covers a multitude of topics. What do you think professionalism looks like in a presenter? Some aspects are seen in presenters who:

- turn up in plenty of time;
- are unflustered by anything that is thrown at them and take things in their stride;
- look the part – are smartly dressed, look alert and are smiling and confident;
- have all the 'assets' of their presentation (slides, script, props, etc) to hand;
- are gracious and polite to everyone they meet at the venue.

Your list may well be longer than this, but what virtually all aspects of professionalism have in common is that they can be 'acquired' by pre-planning. Being alert is about having sufficient sleep the night before; smartness of dress relates to the attention to detail. All of these little details count. Don't be dismissive of the receptionist or the person serving the coffee.

> **Tip**
>
> If you give all of this attention to detail before you get on stage, you are bound to exude a professional demeanour once you start to speak. This is a great credibility builder and audiences love it.

Expertise

Stick to your specialist subject area and you will look and sound confident. You don't necessarily have to spend 20 minutes focused on telling members of the audience why you are so knowledgeable on this topic, they will sense by your air of authority soon enough if you are the genuine article.

If you are talking on a subject you have limited knowledge of, just deliver what you have to and don't start trying to embellish the content with 'false expertise'. If you are forced into handling a question and answer session at the end of such a speech, find a form of words that lets those in the audience know you are not a topic expert, but if you cannot answer their queries right away, you have a team of specialists who will swing into action and get an answer back to them within a day or two.

Charisma

I have left charisma until last, because although it's something I've considered and discussed over many years, I still find it very difficult to define; it feels like one of those 'know it when I see it' things.

There are definitely individuals who we are drawn to, who are 'more attractive' than the average person who we would sit up and take notice of if we heard them speaking. Is charisma something you can define in a logical way though, or is it too much of an emotional quality? As I say, I am not sure of the answer to this one. What I do know is that if you combine all the factors above together, in one package, and add a pinch of your own natural personality, you will have a recipe for charisma, because I honestly believe it is something that can be developed by most of us, even if there are a few people we envy, who seem to have been born with it. I cannot help feeling that by developing your presentation skills you will develop a higher degree of charisma at the same time.

Activity

Think of a great public speaker, either a famous person whose presentation you haven't actually attended or someone you have watched and heard yourself. With the person in mind, draw up your own comprehensive list of the qualities he or she possesses. Try to make these one-word descriptions.

Give yourself a mark out of 10 for each quality, then think about how you could improve that score.

Summary points

- There are lots of great reasons to improve your presentation skills; take some time now and again to review these and remind yourself why you are doing this.

- You might admire other presenters and public speakers, but you cannot be them. It is much better to observe what they do and adapt it to your own personality.

- Be a bit larger than life when you deliver a presentation, as it helps the audience get a sense of your unique personality.

- Understanding the person you are is part of improving yourself in the eyes of your audience.

- Consider some of the attributes of good speakers and think of how these apply to you.

02

Where do you begin?

Not all presentations are the same, so the amount of time and effort you put into preparing and delivering different presentations will vary. How do you keep all that in proportion? Let's have a look at that question, as well as thinking about what opportunities there are to go out and seek speaking engagements proactively.

The work you put into a speech or presentation will, most likely, not be governed by things like the size of the audience or the length of the address. It is much more likely that the importance of the occasion – such as your brother's wedding or a massive sales pitch – and who the audience is will be the deciding factors. Incidentally, this rule will also apply to how nervous you are likely to feel. Often, professional speakers will admit that they are more afraid of a forthcoming speech at a school reunion, in front of 50 old friends, than an hour-long conference address to an audience of 500.

Different types of presentation

I have compiled some notes on the kinds of presentation you might be asked to deliver. These are designed to act as a quick guide, so that you can get the task into perspective and start to take some instant decisions about how you are going to prepare.

The family occasion

I have started with this one as it is the most personal kind of presentation we are called upon to do. It might be as formal as a wedding speech (say, as the father of the bride) or just a few well-chosen words on the occasion of grandma's 80th birthday.

As mentioned earlier, very often we are most nervous for this kind of speech, which is a paradox really, as we are presenting to an audience of people who are already firmly on our side. I have never seen an angry heckler at a wedding – an amusing one, yes.

Humour is, of course, appropriate. For example, in the case of grandma's birthday, who could resist recounting some of her more eccentric moments? However, these occasions are also a time for heartfelt sentiment and it is this bit that unnerves most of us, as we try to make sure we express what we feel and not mess it up. The advice here is to keep the emotional bit short, save it for the end, don't make it too slushy and rehearse it tirelessly until it comes out like you want it to.

Business – internal and informal

This category covers the most common type of presentation – the presentations you give to your peers or colleagues in your organization on an ongoing basis. Here you might expect an audience of up to 50 people and often the purpose will be to impart information and allow for some kind of discussion.

They won't be expecting you to do a full 'song and dance' routine; these are the people who know you well professionally, so you really need to be yourself. However, this does not excuse 'taking them for granted' and giving a below-par performance. Often, the thing that marks one person out for success, over another, is their passion and enthusiasm for the subject. Don't try to manufacture this, but look for the parts of the speech that stir you.

Usually you will have a high degree of control over the environment (the boardroom, or some other similar meeting space), so it won't be necessary to do a full check of the ergonomics of the surroundings. Technical issues shouldn't prove a problem either.

Business – internal and formal

One example is where the boss kindly requests that you deliver a formal address at the annual conference for all staff. Even if you work in a small organization, there is a lot to be learned from preparing for this kind of speech.

Let's say for now that the venue is still an internal one. You are familiar with the room set-up, the necessary technology is all in place and you have access in advance for rehearsal. Most of these things are under your control.

Focus now on the content of what you are going to say, because it is likely to be scrutinized more closely by an audience of knowledgeable peers and colleagues, not to mention your boss. This is a case where you will need to share the content of your address in some detail with other platform speakers, so that you neither duplicate nor contradict each other.

Business external

This category can cover anything from a sales pitch or presentation of your organization's credentials to you being asked to deliver a conference speech at another company's event.

Preparation for this needs to be top notch. You are representing your company and it is also a showcase for you as an individual.

The audience is likely to be polite and respectful – after all you are an invited guest – but don't let that make you complacent. Unlike the internal situations, where you are familiar with the surroundings and equipment, you will now have to put in extra effort to get a working knowledge of what you will be dealing with on someone else's patch. It might also be the case that a third-party venue, such as a hotel or conference centre, has been hired for the occasion. Either way, make sure you do the legwork to understand the technology and the ergonomics of the room, as well as obtaining a full briefing about the members of the audience and their expectations.

Guest speaker

This can be very like the category above, but I have used it in the context of a less formal kind of address, so you might have been asked to give a fairly light-hearted introduction to an event, to act as facilitator or deliver an after-dinner speech.

Shortly, we will look at making opportunities for practising making speeches, which will include volunteering to be guest speaker at local clubs and societies. Just because you are unpaid and the number of people in the audience is generally small, don't treat them with contempt. This is a great training ground, but only if you take it seriously.

If you can prepare some interesting content, you should be able to adapt it for a number of different events, which will help you with the skill of honing your material and give you a good understanding of the elements that work best for you.

These are just some examples. There are bound to be circumstances where you are asked to speak that are not covered here, but I hope there are enough general tips in broad categories for you to be able to pick and choose what will work best, according to the circumstances. Use the preparation matrix (Figure 2.1) as an at a glance guide to how much work you'll need to put in.

The actual content of your speech will be governed by the event itself; these are the nuts and bolts of your address. Combine this

Figure 2.1 Preparation matrix

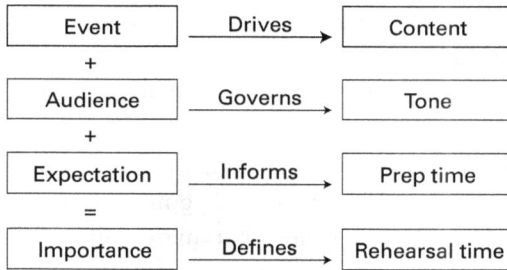

Event	__Drives__ →	Content
+		
Audience	__Governs__ →	Tone
+		
Expectation	__Informs__ →	Prep time
=		
Importance	__Defines__ →	Rehearsal time

with your knowledge of who is in the audience and what their expectation is and you will have a clear idea of the tone to use. Add on the expectation of the organizers and your preparation time in terms of pulling the content together and writing it up will reveal itself. Finally, all these things combined will tell you how important this particular speech is, which in turn will help you scale the amount of rehearsal time to put in.

Desperately seeking speaking

Never stop improving on your presentation technique. I just cannot emphasize enough the need for practice – that's what really makes one speaker stand out from the next and if confidence building is what you are trying to achieve, what could be better than having lots of chances to try out your skills?

But where do you start? What opportunities are there to hone your skills? The answer is to start small and be proactive.

The strange thing about audience size is that most speakers don't pay much attention to it once it gets above a certain number. 'Dying' on stage is just as horrible in front of 50 as 500 people. At first, there is a kind of psychological fear that might increase in line with the size of the crowd, but soon enough you just get used to the fact that there are 'some' people out there; it could be a few or many.

I can't emphasise strongly enough the significance of practice here. The more times you're in front of a crowd, the less bothered you are by it's size. Eventually, your confidence grows so much, that you welcome bigger audiences with a 'more the merrier' attitude.

Every town has its own collection of societies and clubs with special interests and their regular meetings can be much enlivened by the services of a willing, interesting and, most importantly, free speaker. Start by identifying what is going on around you. Are there women's interest groups that meet regularly, business or charitable societies, events that are based on hobbies, such as for photographers, gardeners or bird-watchers? Next, try to map your own interests and/or experiences to the things that might resonate with the group. What have you done in your life that makes a great story? It can be anything really, because it is not the topic that matters, but the opportunity to increase your presentation 'flying hours'.

Some groups will have a set format and will expect you to tie in with that, but most are fairly informal and are happy to go with what you suggest, as long as it is reasonable. Plan to present for around 20 to 30 minutes. Try to keep the content interesting. A 'show and tell', where you take some physical object with you that the audience can examine, is always a good idea. There is usually an expectation that you will finish with a question and answer session.

Always ask for feedback from your host after the event and add that person's opinion to your own feeling of what went well, or not so well. Use this information to help you improve.

Set a realistic target of, say, making one speech a month. It might mean that after a while you will need to start travelling further afield, but often this happens anyway, as you are recommended by your first group to an adjacent one. Build up a file containing details of what you said to each group, when and where and also the contact details of the person at the society or club who booked you. When you have developed new material, you will be able to make a second approach and will be welcomed with open arms, if you delivered well in the first place. These are also the kind of people who might be prepared to give you a glowing testimonial when you are chasing future bookings.

Even closer to home there are occasions in most social circles when it is appropriate for someone to deliver what my old man used to call 'a few well-chosen words'. Engagements, big birthdays (especially those marking decades), milestone anniversaries and christenings are all the kind of occasion when people often appreciate someone marking it with a short speech. Never let an opportunity to be 'on your feet' slip by.

In these early stages, it is a good idea to develop a bank of different topics to speak on. This will increase your chances of being asked to present and has the added benefit of giving you lots of practice at writing new material.

Activity

Spend 30 minutes tracking down a list of what's on in your locality. Think about the kind of societies mentioned in this chapter and use different sources, including social media, internet, personal contacts with friends and neighbours, to draw up a list. Choose the top three organizations that you think you could approach and find out their policy regarding speakers. Based on what you discover, map out a plan of action to secure a speaking engagement within the next month.

Summary points

- Make quick judgements about the sort of presentation you have been asked to do, so that you can put an appropriate amount of time and effort into it.

- Consider the importance of the speech to you, rather than just looking at the size of the audience or the prestige of the event.

- Actively seek out local opportunities to get you started on the speaker circuit; compile a file containing contact details and the requirements of each group.

- Keep as much variety in your content as possible. This will expose you to a much greater range of audiences.

- Stay alert to new opportunities, don't be a shrinking violet and be sure to volunteer for any speaking engagement you can.

03

What on earth are you going to say?

When you are an aspiring speaker, you may see a presenter with the enviable ability to make what seems a spontaneous, unscripted speech, full of heartfelt sentiment, wit and articulate observation. The truth of the matter is that, mostly, it has been written and rehearsed in advance, giving it the appearance of being off the cuff. In this chapter we are going to start looking at a process to begin your writing, so that you can make the most of the new speaking opportunities you are seeking. It is sometimes difficult to know where to begin, so as a starting point here are some general rules.

Start with the audience

Before you even think of putting pen to paper, you have to consider the most important people in this whole process: the members of the audience. However fascinating your subject matter is to you, the acid test is whether you engage the people you are delivering to. Nothing else matters as much.

With some presentations, such as an internal company one, you will be able to gauge the crowd accurately, because of your intimate knowledge of how the organization works and its culture.

However, once you step out in the big wide world, you will be making guesses about who the members of the audience are and about their expectations. Contrast the attitudes and psyche contained in a room full of primary school teachers with those of the teenage children of city bankers. Although you could probably make some assumptions about both, you might be surprised by some of the realities. The lesson is, if possible, try to speak to a few of these people before you put pen to paper. If you can find out what their lives are like, their loves and hates, problems and passions, then you will find it much easier to write in a way that appeals to them.

In the absence of this kind of personal research, do your best to get hold of a delegate list in advance. Sometimes, at business events, the job title of each delegate will appear on the list too, providing you with information about their seniority and the type of job they do. All of this is useful in compiling a picture of what they are like. The danger of no knowledge, is that you will simply 'broadcast' your speech, rather than 'involve and engage' your listeners.

Develop templates

Everyone will tell you that no two presentations are the same and it is most definitely the case that we should do our best to take account of a different audience, the dynamics of a room, the mood and atmosphere. That said, having some standard material that can be adapted across a range of presentations is a good thing too.

Good idea

When you are writing, rehearsing and delivering your speeches, think about how different elements can be adapted for other presentations. Do you have a killer opening that, with a bit of thought, could be used on different occasions? A good example of this might be a generic story about yourself, or an issue that you feel passionate about – the environment, respect in society, the need for strong leadership, releasing people's potential (it's up to you) – which you can use as a lead in to whatever you have been asked to speak about.

The same is true of stories. Often, a good anecdote will stand alone and might easily be related to a range of topics that you are called upon to cover. I have a friend in his seventies who had a long and successful career as a stand-up comedian. He once told me that he only ever had three opening lines to a show; they were his 'go to' and they never let him down.

Topicality

Being up to the minute with your topic is a great way of showing members of your audience how 'in touch' you are, with the added bonus that they are likely to have been concerned about the same thing themselves, very recently. Keep abreast of what's happening in the news, nationally and internationally. Don't ignore trivia – a good topical joke about a celebrity story or a soap opera plot line will really engage the right audience – and consider major themes that are relevant to your topic and the world at large. It's best to stick with the light-hearted; heavy political or social comment risks dividing your audience. Even when you think everyone thinks like you, it can be quite a shock to find they don't, and the last place you want that to happen is in a public forum where all eyes are on you.

There are also some personal topics that will always be relevant and have a universal appeal. Often these are centred around relationships, but remember to be careful to gauge the age and lifestyle of your audience before you launch into your anecdote; stories about children always go down well, especially if you have an endearing toddler story or a frustrating teenager one. Most of us can think of a time when our parents drove us mad, so that might be appropriate too. Work-based topics could fit the bill, especially if the experience is a common one, like too many meetings, or e-mail overload.

Active research and statistical information

There is a raft of information you can gather that will contribute towards excellent future presentations. Do a self-audit, where you consider the type of subjects you are most often asked to talk about, then set aside time to find out some interesting facts. Statistics are good and carry great weight, but only if they are simple to digest; a long list of figures will only serve to baffle an audience and an overloaded slide, full of data, will do the same. It is also increasingly the case, in an age of supposed 'fake news', that statistics tend to be questioned more than ever in terms of their relative 'truth'.

Try to stick to everyday issues – things that people can relate to. An example is the way that presenters often represent the size of something, relating it to 'equivalent to the area of four football pitches'. Where possible, try to find your own unique way of describing things, rather than relying on what has gone before.

Quirky 'facts' are equally good, and yes, the quotation marks do imply that the truth may have been bent a little. I am not advocating out-and-out lying, but by the way you present something your audience will often be forgiving if you use the adage 'never let the facts get in the way of a good story'. An example might be: 'Today, there is more computing power in a singing birthday card than there was in the entire world in 1958.' Even the most pedantic audience member is unlikely to take you to task over whether this is true or not. The point is, you're making a point! Your audience will quickly engage and understand you are illustrating how quickly, dynamically and massively technology has moved on, in a short space of time.

Individuality

If you buy in to the idea that an audience wants to hear you speak because you are unique, you can start to amass a file of material that reflects your own interests and personality. Developing an eye for what might be useful in future is about combining your past experience with the knowledge of what you aspire to present upon, some way down the line. News clippings, cartoons, facts and figures can all be amassed and kept in your own 'presenter's box file'.

I'm rather 'old school' and like the physical assets, so I've got dozens of Post-it Notes and scores of actual clippings filed away. In more recent times I've begun to collect these electronically, with a file on my desktop labelled 'vital info'. As well as a pile of documents containing relevant bits of text, there is also a section full of URLs and social media followers for online content that has impressed me.

Good idea

Keep a high level of awareness of all you 'consume' – stupid things our politicians have said on a news channel or a snippet of conversation overheard at a railway station are equally valid. With the material in the public domain, we can often go and look it up again later. All the best gaffes appear on YouTube, or similar sites, at some time or another. However, with the overheard snippet of conversation, jotting down the relevant comment and filing it away for future use will pay great dividends, not least because it is likely to be unique to you and a reflection of how your personality sees the world.

Apart from the obvious benefit of having your 'presentation preparation muscles' exercised, you will be surprised at how useful your box file is in the future, when you sit down with a blank sheet of paper to write a new presentation. Often a piece of information that you have squirrelled away in the past will help to illustrate a point you want to make; occasionally, you might pick up a gem that is so good it can form the central core of everything you want to say.

The materials you collect are up to you. They need to have a personal resonance, otherwise you will lack conviction when you are presenting them. Remember when using any of this type of material to observe the principles of copyright law and seek permission from the instigator in advance and/or credit the original source.

Using quotations

Quotations are a marvellous way of illustrating a point in a presentation, but only if they are chosen carefully, delivered skilfully and timed to coincide with the point you are trying to make. Strip the quote bare, uncover its real meaning and only then can you decide if it fits with your own content. An irrelevant quotation is worse than not using one at all. How you deliver a quotation is just as important; if you slip it in seamlessly, people will be more impressed than if you make a big thing of it.

It is worth emphasizing the need to consider the members of your audience and how important it is to connect with them. For example, bear in mind that displaying the literary prowess you gathered during your privileged education might just risk alienating one or two people.

As far as sources of quotations are concerned, life could not be easier. It used to be that you had to be tremendously well read to be able to deliver an insightful bit of wisdom from the classics of literature, now you just use a search engine. Ironically, when you are looking for a killer quote that fits the bill for today's presentation, you inevitably uncover all sorts of gems that are just not appropriate right now. Make sure you save them in your 'favourites', or set up a separate text document that you can index, according to subject.

Be careful with length and complexity. The best examples to use are the ones that are easy to grasp: the one-liners. If your chosen quotation is longer than that, it had better be making a substantial point and one that your audience will be able to follow.

Figure 3.1 summarizes some good starting points to develop your content. Note that whatever you do, make sure you consider the think bubble about audience *before* anything else.

Figure 3.1   Content starters

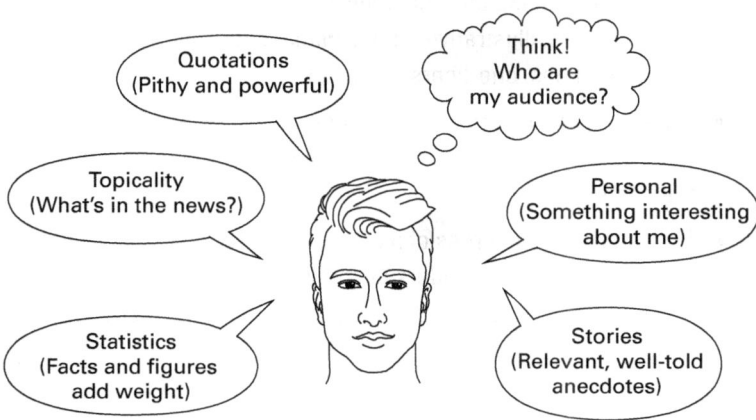

Activity

Over the next week, make a conscious effort to start your presenter's content kit by seeking out some relevant items that you can begin to collect. Add good old-fashioned newspapers and specialist magazines to your favourite 'socials'. Set yourself a target of a minimum of five quotations and three interesting articles.

Summary points

- Don't even begin to write until you have considered who the members of the audience will be. Find out as much as you can about them, right at the start.

- Tailor some content to the specific audience, but also keep generic material in mind that you can use across a variety of speeches.

- Stay alert to all the different things you can put in future presentations: illustrative stories with a good moral at the end, quotations, one-liners and jokes.

- When you come across great quotations, make sure you write them down or note where they came from so you can find them later.

- Bookmark good sources of material on social media and keep separate 'favourites' folders by topic heading.

04
It's time to write... now!

So far we have looked at how to collect ideas together and at some of the factors that will influence your writing. I don't think we can put off the business of putting pen to paper any longer. This chapter begins by looking at how closely scripted you want your presentation to be and what medium you will use when presenting, then it moves on to look at five steps to writing a presentation.

Thinking about all the things you could say is rather different from sitting down and writing the presentation. Before you can begin, you need to decide on the level of scripting versus spontaneity. Figure 4.1, a matrix of risks and rewards, outlines some of the potential pitfalls depending on your level of scripting, balancing this with the upside of when it works well.

Figure 4.1 Risks and rewards

	Off the cuff	Off the script
+	Heartfelt Personal Passionate Admirable	Accurate Articulate Planned Structured
−	Incomplete Shambolic Stilted Inaccurate	Robotic Unfeeling Insincere Unemotional

The big script

For the novice or the very nervous, the only form that the presenter is likely to feel comfortable with is the word-for-word script. If you are just starting out on the speaker circuit and are worried about forgetting something vitally important, this kind of scripting has its place. The upside is that you can stop worrying about what you are going to say, it is all there in front of you. The corresponding downside is that it is very hard to make this kind of presentation flow in a natural way.

In a business setting members of the audience might want to see a bit more spontaneity.

Write it, learn it

This is at the opposite end of the spectrum. For a really important presentation you might decide that you want to talk without holding a script or referring to notes of any kind. In this case you have no alternative but to write the speech long hand, learn it word for word and deliver it. It is tough and there is no shortcut, plus the fact that without cues you risk forgetting something or losing your thread, but the truth is that it looks fantastic if you can pull it off.

Notes and nudges

Somewhere between the two previous scenarios lies the middle ground occupied by a variety of notes, nudges and cues: the signals that connect the narrative together. This is where most presentations lie, giving a good balance of security (because you don't have to remember the whole presentation) and an 'easy', flowing speech (as long as you have rehearsed properly).

Two really good pieces of 'hardware' for helping to deliver this are cue cards and PowerPoint. The might sound rather old school, but they still work. It is better if you don't try to use them together, otherwise you can get confused as to where you are. In the process of writing and rehearsing your presentation there is a funnel effect. When you first get started and are mapping out the content in detail, the cuing device (cards or PowerPoint slides) will contain a lot of information, so that you can follow the flow. However, as you hone down your story, you will be able to weed out any unnecessary words and phrases, relying only on the next memory jogger to move things on.

Cue cards

The great advantage of using cue cards instead of an A4 script is that you don't have it flapping about in front of you, distracting your audience and causing you stress as you wonder if you have the pages in the right order. As it is less obtrusive, there is a greater likelihood of your speech looking spontaneous. I have known professional presenters who use their cue cards more as a 'comfort blanket' than a script – something to refer to in case of emergency, such as total memory loss.

Tip

Use cards of around 12 cm × 8 cm, normally the kind you would have in a card index system. These are about the smallest you can get, but they will fit in a pocket until you are ready to deliver your speech, and if kept in the palm of your hand, the audience will hardly notice they are there.

How you lay out the card is up to you, but I've included an example. You will notice that the card is numbered in the middle and I always use both sides, to reduce the total number of cards I am carrying. I make it a rule to flip the cards over top to bottom, so the notes on the reverse side are upside down until you flip the card (unlike a book, the pages of which you turn side to side).

Figure 4.2 An example cue card

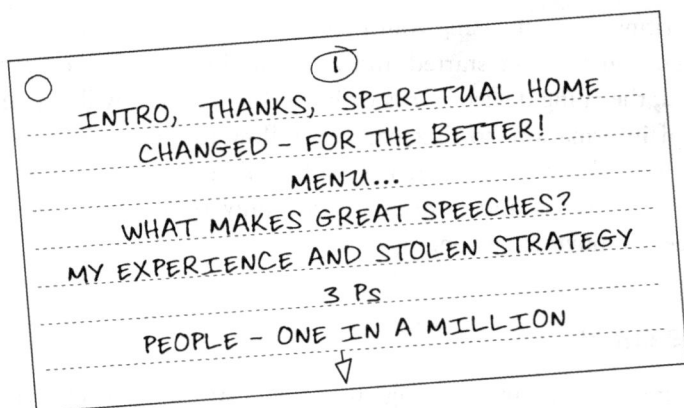

```
            (1)
INTRO, THANKS, SPIRITUAL HOME
    CHANGED - FOR THE BETTER!
           MENU...
    WHAT MAKES GREAT SPEECHES?
MY EXPERIENCE AND STOLEN STRATEGY
           3 Ps
    PEOPLE - ONE IN A MILLION
              ↓
```

It doesn't really matter which way you choose to do this, just be consistent, so that once you are in the swing of using cards they will always be formatted in the same way.

Very often when I've been teaching presentation skills face to face I've suggested the use of cue cards, and I've lost count of the times people have simply transferred their full script onto a great wad of cards. This is worse than useless, because when you lose your way in the presentation, you won't have a chance of finding the right bit on the right card. Take note of the example above and condense your content down; remember, these are prompts only.

Writing with PowerPoint

The significant difference between using PowerPoint and cards is that when using PowerPoint you will be sharing the cues with your audience as you go along.

Most experts will tell you not to put too much information on your slides and you should certainly never reveal the whole story on them, otherwise the audience wouldn't need you there to explain it. You might chose to write bullet points that are a little bit cryptic, but don't make them so weird that your audience cannot see the connection between the bullet point and what you are saying.

Good idea

Try compiling a presentation where each slide contains just a single word. This is not only an interesting exercise, but also good practice for keeping the content of your slides brief.

Once you have decided which of the above methods you are going to use, you can begin the process of writing. One final aspect to consider before you start, is to think about structure.

- First, tell them what you are going to tell them. This sets up the presentation and manages the audience's expectations. It also 'trails' what's coming up.
- Tell them (present the ideas that you have just outlined).
- Finish by telling them what you have told them (reviewing and summarizing the central message that you have put across).

Working to this formula will ensure that your presentation has a logical beginning, middle and end. This kind of signposting also keeps audiences engaged and is part of any good presentation.

Activity

Watch any 30-minute news bulletin. It will follow a similar formula, opening with the headlines, followed by more detail on each story in order. Around 12 minutes into the bulletin the newscaster will pause to sum up the main stories and signpost a 'coming up...' section. Before the bulletin ends, a similar review of top stories will round things off. This is a great discipline for a half-hour presentation.

Coming up is a five-step approach to writing a presentation. To illustrate the process. The chosen topic is, 'What makes great speeches?'

The five steps to good writing

The big idea

Don't be intimidated by the blank sheet of paper, or screen, in front of you and wonder how you are going to fill your time slot. Once you get going, it is the editing down that is often the problem.

Start with a 'big idea'. Sometimes this is given to you as the subject of your speech; on other occasions, you will be expected to come up with it yourself.

The 'big idea' for the speech in this example is to outline the 3 Ps of great speech making.

Three main points

The 'list of three' rule has really gained momentum over recent years. Limiting yourself to three points allows you to focus your mind on a small number of issues, not least because it makes them easier to remember and it introduces a level of discipline where you have to be ruthless in your editing of content.

Let's look at the three main points I have chosen for this speech:

- preparation;
- practice;
- people.

The use of alliteration is deliberate. It might sound a bit of a cliché, but the truth is that when the points are spoken aloud, one after another, it gives a memory hook for the audience. It also helps you recall them as you present.

Brainstorming the main points

Now that I have decided on the important areas I am going to cover, I need to be thinking of the sub-points I wish to make about each. Below is the kind of list I would generate for each of my three Ps.

Preparation

- Good speeches are the product of a lot of hard work in advance.
- An audience deserves to be treated with respect, so you need to prepare.
- There are many elements to a speech; they all need to be considered.
- Once the speech is written you will want to see where it will be delivered:
  - Room ergonomics are important.
  - Technical equipment is vital.
- Timing and length of the address need to be considered.

Practice

- Even professionals need to rehearse.
- Sounding confident is all about knowing your script.
- Listening back to a speech allows you the opportunity to edit and hone it.
- The more rehearsed you are, the more relaxed you will be.
- Being relaxed will help you deal with the unexpected.

People

- Human interaction is what makes us remember great speeches.
- How the members of the audience 'feel' about the content depends on their reaction to the speaker.

- Part of all good speeches is persuasion. Only people can do that.
- Great speakers really engage with their audience.
- Each of us is unique; so, by association, is every speech.

Developing the headings

Using these brainstormed ideas, the next stage is to think about what you will say on each sub-point. It doesn't matter too much if there are some bullet points that are more substantial than others, the weaker ones will be dropped in the editing stage.

The next part of the process involves weaving these things together, so they make sense.

The five-step plan outlined above for speech writing is a guide to get you started. This is because, for many of us, just putting the initial ideas down is the hardest part.

I sometimes think a good analogy for writing is sculpture. You start with something that is vaguely the shape of the final piece, then mould it and refine it until it is ready to be presented to an audience.

Activity

Write something! Exercising your writing muscles is good practice for when you will have to compile a real presentation. Think of a topic you feel strongly about and sketch out the notes for a short presentation on it. If you struggle to think of a suitable topic, find out today's news headlines and develop a short speech that would outline what's happening in one of the stories. Take about half an hour on this, then if you are inspired repeat the exercise using a different topic.

Summary points

- Before you sit down to write, decide how you intend to deliver your address, as this will influence how you approach the task.

- Get some ideas down on paper. Procrastination is the enemy of the writer.

- Use a staged process that has a logical flow. Either follow the five-step plan in this chapter or find something else that works for you.

- Lists of three work well when you are speaking. This can also help to make the writing stage easier, as it limits the number of ideas you will work on.

- Try to sustain a narrative through your writing as this will help the presentation flow and remind you of what comes next.

05
The power of storytelling

Before we were able to write things down, it was important to be able to pass on the learning of one generation to the next and so this was done by telling true, or illustrative, stories. Often there was a moral to the tale and this was there for a reason. Before society had developed formal law and order, there needed to be some code of values by which we lived, so stories always made some kind of a point at the end.

If we examine many of the fairy tales that are still told today, the key learning from them is as important as ever. However, there is another good reason why we pass on the learning in this particular format and that is because it is memorable; the learning is embedded in the narrative.

These two essential constructs of good stories, moral and memorability, make them an ideal vehicle for putting your points across in a presentation, where the audience may have nothing to take away at the end other than the experience of having listened to you. I can bear witness to the power of storytelling, as I can still recall anecdotes that I heard presenters tell 20 or more years ago – which is some feat, as I often cannot remember my own PIN number.

The benefits of storytelling

Storytelling offers these benefits in the context of a presentation:

- It helps you to illustrate your point. Some content can be dull and audiences might not engage with it very well, but a good story, well-chosen and delivered, can bring the issue to life and capture fresh interest.

- You can make a long-term impact with storytelling; the very fact that people might be able to recall what you told them in story form, much later on, shows that your presentation has the ability to affect behaviours or attitudes far into the future.

- A story adds to your popularity. It makes life easier for the members of your audience, so they will be much more prepared to listen to your whole presentation.

- Stories can make you seem more human. Really good presenters often have a clutch of stories that they tell 'against' themselves. Showing our own frailty says to an audience that we are all fallible; we are all in this together.

- A story brings light and shade. When the content you are delivering is heavy going, it is great to be able to lighten the mood with a good story.

- Stories provide you with anchors. Make sure the stories you choose are relevant to the rest of your content and you will have much less trouble remembering your speech. You might simply recall the stories, but then build upon them – you will have a ready-made outline.

- Storytelling can add to your confidence. Having some tried and trusted elements of presentation to fall back on is a great confidence booster; for example, I have a good 'technology' story that is a real banker if the PowerPoint ever fails. The added benefit is that while I spin it out, there is just a chance that a technical expert will get me up and running again!

So, stories have many benefits when we are presenting, but where do they come from and how do we collect them?

Collecting stories

> ### Good idea
>
> Other speakers whose live presentations you have seen, or who you have watched recordings of, can be a good source of stories. Search online for these stories. Books and journals often contain excellent anecdotes and trade magazine articles are useful too. If you work in a specialist area, such as customer service or HR, subscribe to the relevant publications and social media feeds for detailed information about your profession.
>
> Stay interested in other people too. Ask open questions about their background and how they got to where they are.
>
> Even eavesdropping on a bus can yield a great story – just ask my mum!

Good stories are everywhere and even if they are not particularly relevant when you hear or read them, you know better than anybody the kind of speeches you are asked to deliver, so can start to build up a bank of stories for the future.

Of course, with any of these sources, it helps to know what you are looking for. Here is a quick list of a few business topics that might one day be relevant to your speech. As you meander through life, capture any stories you come across that might be handy later on.

Hot business issues

- Artificial Intelligence – collect stories on the pace of change, our inability to use technology, how powerful AI has become, where it might take us next and how we respond to it.

Figure 5.1   Elements of a story

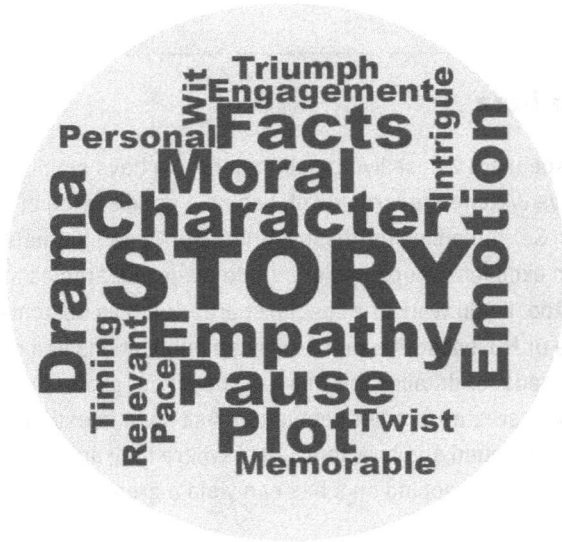

- Economy – use stories that consider the state of the nation's finances; how you budget in your household; the fact that the more you have, the more you spend; whether we're in boom or bust – how you can tell.

- Conflict – issues include being made redundant, sacking people, boardroom battles, arguments in meetings, people who say 'with the greatest respect' when it is the last thing they mean, the stress of handling difficult situations.

- Compliance – areas for stories might be the burden of 'health and safety' legislation, the hoops we have to jump through, corporate social responsibility – why it is right to do the right thing, the pitfalls of non-compliance, changes in legislation.

- Communications – look out for stories about the burden of e-mail, using technology on the move, how ambiguity creeps in, communication breakdowns, the benefits and downsides of social networking, the astounding march of AI.

- Achievement – what it is like to win, hitting targets and how that feels, setting goals and living them, what success means to you, planning the future, handling disappointment, resilience to 'bouncing back'.

How to tell a story

There is quite an art to telling a story well and if you are going to make it work for you, then delivery is all important.

Top tips for improving delivery

- **Know the story**
  This sounds obvious, doesn't it? However, we have all been in a social situation where a husband and wife have interrupted each other during the telling of a story as one of them was 'getting it wrong'. Stories have a narrative thread running through them and to make sense you have to follow the sequence in order, otherwise you will lose your audience.

- **Stick to the 'facts'**
  Whether fact or fiction, the important lesson is to tell what is relevant and leave all the other stuff to one side. Some people meander through a story with one digression after another, so that by the time they get to the end, you are simply dazed and confused.

- **Paint a picture**
  Your words aren't all you have when telling stories, fill in the kind of detail that will give your listeners a real sense of what was happening and emphasize this with body language. If you were telling a tale of attending a lavish wedding, you might say

things like 'champagne on tap', 'massive marquee' or 'palatial surroundings', just to bring the tale to life.

- **Develop the characters**
  Good stories often involve great characters, so give a sense of who these people are. Again, the picture-painting technique of the previous point will come in handy. Include characteristics that are pertinent, so a sporting story would contain physical attributes, with phrases such as 'a man mountain' or 'fast as a greyhound'. A 'human' story might focus on more emotional elements, including comments such as 'so kind-hearted' or 'generous and thoughtful'.

- **Use 'timing'**
  The pace and verbal delivery of a story can really add to its value. Think about the difference between telling a ghost story to a child or recounting the tale of a sales pitch to a work colleague. Tone of voice, speed, variation and sense of drama will change according to circumstances. Don't be afraid during a presentation to add some dramatic touches to your delivery. With practice, they will enhance a good story even further.

- **Go beyond**
  Apart from the basic constructs of the story itself, what is it saying? There may be an obvious moral at the end, but if not, be prepared to spell it out. In a presentational context, you need to be able to relate your story directly to the content you are delivering.

- **Practise**
  If you are thinking of using a story in a presentation, look for opportunities to give it a few 'dry runs' to see if it works. In a smaller gathering, perhaps socially in the bar after work.

Activity

Write three stories about things that have happened to you, using just 50 words to summarize each. The topics are as follows: 'That's when I knew it had all gone wrong', 'Oh, the benefits of youth!' and 'My hero'.

Summary points

- Storytelling is an age-old way of embedding learning; people remember good stories forever.

- A well-chosen anecdote can add weight to your argument, both on a logical level and in an emotional sense.

- Practise turning your observations of human nature into stories, as these are the kind that resonate most with a variety of audiences.

- Compile a mental list of topics and start collecting stories about them. They will provide a springboard to your writing in the future.

- Use every opportunity to have a go at storytelling. The improvement in your technique will amaze you.

06
Using humour

Being funny can be the best way of making a terrific presentation. I say 'can be' because humour is like dynamite – fantastic if it explodes in a spectacular display of fireworks, less good if it goes off in your face. This chapter follows on from those on writing and storytelling as the subjects are interrelated. It can be that humour is truly spontaneous, a reaction to something that happens on the day, but more of that later; for now, some guidance on how to amuse your audience.

Appropriateness

The first rule of humour is to question whether it is appropriate. All the things we have so far considered about audiences, the type of presentation you have been asked to give, the prevailing mood at the time and the circumstances of the speech are important.

I think there are very few occasions where some form of humour cannot help to put your message across. Just because you are delivering 'dry' content about the company's annual accounts, for example, doesn't mean you cannot throw in the odd one-liner, if only to check that the audience is still awake. In business, it is often the case that people can find amusement in the darker side of an issue. Here is a great example.

Humour in times of adversity

The term 'gallows humour' conveys the idea of wit in times of adversity! This type of humour exists to a greater or lesser extent in all organizations. When the going gets tough, often the only way to cope is to laugh it off. For most of us, that's about tight deadlines, over work, competitive markets, economic conditions, redundancy, or clashes of personality.

However, in some walks of life, the daily stresses are much more acute and it is here where humour is the greatest coping mechanism. Few of us (fortunately), have to deal with death and destruction on a daily basis, but those in the armed forces, the emergency services and associated organizations face up to such things as part of their job role. The things that firefighters see, the trauma witnessed by A & E nurses, the grief seen by funeral directors – all these things would be impossible to cope with if it were not for humour. It may be judged as inappropriate from the outside, but as the saying goes, 'if you didn't laugh, you'd cry'.

When it comes to good taste, stay well on the 'safe' side of the line. If there is any chance you might offend with a remark, then don't say it.

The flip side of the appropriateness coin is that there may be some circumstances where humour is not only appropriate, but virtually essential. If you are trying to enthuse an audience and have been asked to deliver a 'rallying cry', it will be much better received if you are able to do it with a bit of wit thrown in. Equally, if an audience is being expected to listen to a full day of platform speakers and the rest of them haven't raised a titter, it is all the more important that you are able to lift the mood a bit.

Are you funny?

Appropriateness is one very important criterion to use when thinking about whether or not to attempt humour. Another one is your chance of success.

All of us are funny in our own way. We all have times when we make others laugh, but controlling this and delivering it, to order, is another thing entirely. In the movie *White Christmas* actor Danny Kaye delivers the line (when talking about himself), 'I know this guy, he's kinda funny in living rooms...', which helps to sum up the contextual nature of humour.

There is an acid test that applies to humour – and it's pretty hard to argue with. Do members of the audience laugh? If they don't, you are not funny, so bear this in mind the next time you think you have a killer line or hilarious story.

Even top comics have to work hard to get their humour to be funny. One of the current crop of British funny men recently admitted to spending six hours a day working on his material and yet when he (or his peers) crack a one-liner, we think they have just thought of it.

Planned versus off the cuff

I love the expression 'a well-rehearsed ad-lib'. For me it sums up the nature of comedy – that when it is done well, it really does appear to have been made up there and then. As just outlined, virtually all good comedy is meticulously planned.

If you witness a really good business presenter doing the same address twice, you might be surprised at how much of the content, which appeared spontaneous first time around, is actually incorporated in the second address. Comedians call it 'working the material'. It's a good lesson in business too.

The more planning you do, the better your real ad-libbing becomes. This is mainly driven by having the confidence to attempt a punchline that has just occurred to you, safe in the knowledge that if it doesn't work, you still have your practised material to fall back on.

No one can tell you how to be funny off the cuff. If it comes to you, it comes to you; if not, you cannot force it. Having said all that, if you keep your eyes open to the absurd, if you are prepared to use self-deprecating humour – which I would recommend – then there are often situations when you will simply spot a comedy element in what is happening around you.

What to expect when you deliver a funny line

In professional comedy circles there is a technique called 'riding the gag'. Essentially, it means that you should never look as if you are expecting a laugh. Instead, you just carry on regardless and only pause if the amount of noise makes your next line inaudible. This changes the dynamic between you and the audience from one of 'Look at me, aren't I funny?'(which happens if you deliver the punchline, stop and wait for the audience to laugh) to one of 'Gosh, what a surprise, you found that funny.'

You can see this in action for yourself if you look out for it the next time a comic appears on television. Contrast this technique with Jim Henson's Muppet creation Fozzie Bear, a supposed comic, who would deliver a line and await his laughter. Poor Fozzie usually 'died' on stage at the hands of aged theatre-goers and professional hecklers, Stadler and Waldorf. This is to be avoided if possible.

Jokes versus anecdotes

A good joke, delivered well, at an appropriate part of a presentation, in keeping with the rest of the content and in tune with the kind of audience before you is a fantastic way to endear yourself. But – and you've guessed it, it's a big 'but' – there is a lot of risk associated with jokes.

It is usually pretty obvious that you are purposely telling a gag, making it much harder to 'ride it'. By contrast, if you tell a story, especially one against yourself with an ending that (you hope) will amuse, you can keep on going, only stopping if the audience gets it.

What to do when humour fails

The next thing about jokes is that they are not all funny and what makes one person or group laugh might leave another cold. If this happens, the resulting silence is an awful thing to contend with, but you just have to carry on regardless. Don't draw attention to the lack of laughter, just keep going and hope that when viewed as a whole, no one will remember your one moment of embarrassment during the presentation.

Jokes 'do the rounds', so you forever run the risk that the audience have heard a joke before. In most cases, the nature of a joke that leads to a punchline (which, technically speaking, works because it is unexpected) means that it is never as funny second time around.

Even funny jokes are not worth telling during a presentation unless you can relate them to the rest of the content. The members of the audience may enjoy the light-hearted intervention, but will end up asking themselves what point you were trying to make.

Finally, jokes have a kind of context. In a club, late at night, when people are relaxing with friends and may even have had a drink or two, they are ready to laugh. First thing in the morning, at a conference, with a hangover, they may be less so. Be warned!

The art of exaggeration

The wackier and more exaggerated a story, the greater the likelihood of getting a laugh, so you might begin with the bare bones of a real story, but blow certain aspects up to make them ridiculous. Often, people in an audience can spot themselves in this and presenting a larger-than-life version is a great comedic ploy. For example, being an obsessive list maker is a more common trait than you might expect. When you start talking about how you have a master list of all your other lists, it is funny, and in my case, also happens to be true!

Topicality

A topical story is not necessarily funnier than other stories, but it does have the added benefit of showing that you are 'on the ball' – that you know what's happening in the world and are quick-witted enough to be able to make some kind of humorous reference to it.

Tip

It is worth thinking about the 'world' that the audience is living in. Some of the knowledge will be the common ground, which we all share, such as news and current affairs stories, but it will probably extend beyond to celebrity gossip, knowledge of sporting events or the plot of the current soap operas. Apart from what's happening on a world stage, take your topicality down to a local level too. Find out what people in your audience are thinking about. If presenting within an organization, find out, for example: is the company undergoing expansion? Have those in the audience just won a major piece of business? Are they relocating to plush new offices? Whatever is on their day-to-day agenda is material for topical humour.

In conclusion, there simply is no better way of getting the members of an audience on your side than through the use of humour. They will warm to you, listen more attentively to the rest of your presentation and, as a consequence, remember a greater amount of what you say.

For this reason, I would urge you to use your natural humour as much as you can. Don't force it, feed it in gently, a bit at a time, until you are confident with it, and whatever you do, never look as if you were expecting a laugh. When it comes though, you can accept it gracefully.

Activity

Think of something you are sometimes criticized for. This is the starting point for a story that is self-deprecating. Is it your sense of direction, inability to master technology or obsessive tidiness? Now consider an extreme situation, tailored to whatever the trait is. What was it that drove other people mad about it? How did it resolve itself? What did you learn? Where possible, try to make the witty anecdote something other people would relate to; either as the 'perpetrator' (appealing to all the obsessively tidy people in the audience, for example) or the 'victim' (which will resonate with all those who live with a tidy person).

Summary points

- Funny is good! The most popular presenters are the ones who make their audiences laugh; it is the best way of engaging.

- As always, think about the audience. Don't even consider delivering a story or joke until you have worked out who will be hearing it.

- Ride the gag. Don't look as if you are waiting for a laugh, if it doesn't come, just keep going.

- Begin with stories; they are safer. If you master this art and are brave enough, move on to telling jokes, but make them relevant.

- Look for topical humour on the day of the presentation. What's in the news that morning? What is preoccupying the minds of the people in your audience?

07
Working from home

The seismic shift towards working from home in recent times was, originally, accelerated by the Covid pandemic, but I'd argue that it was coming anyway, and for very many workers, it has simply become 'business as usual'. There are so many reasons why remote working can and does work, across a wide range of different job roles, that it was only a matter of time before this happened.

What no one prepared us for was how to conduct ourselves in this 'new' medium. But, as humans always do, we learned quickly – at least some of us did. A precursor to us being 'forced' on screen by circumstances was the advent of the TikTok generation who chose to do it of their own free will.

In today's world, being on screen is no longer a big thing. It's a daily occurence; it's how influencers make their living and attract millions of aspirational followers; it is in fact the norm.

Rules for better Zooms

For the sake of shorthand, I'll mostly refer to the business platforms as 'Zoom', although Teams, Facetime and plenty of others are available; they all do the same thing, connect people through sound and vision. Later in this book I talk about becoming a control freak and how it helps in the presenter's ongoing battle with confidence. There are two fundamental elements of this when it comes to presenting yourself on screen. Firstly, make sure you know how the tool works, not just the basics of how to mute and un-mute yourself, turn the camera on and off, display other participants on screen, etc, but the new features that are constantly being added, and be early, not just 'on time' or 'a few minutes behind schedule'. The second thing is, if others can see you 'in the waiting room', it already signals that you're keen.

I recently heard the following adage: 'on time is late – early is punctual'. It costs nothing to be early for a Zoom meeting; until it actually starts, no one can see you, so you can be multitasking right down to the wire.

Here are some Zoom rules to follow, which will help you look even better.

Zoom is no different to your office... except

When circumstances forced many organizations to rethink how they worked, the move to Zoom generally came with no additional training, so we found our own way through it. Although you could, in the short term, go 'viral' for having your toddler appear round the door, or the cat slink across your desk, it's hardly the most professional image.

Find a dedicated 'Zoom space', the plainer and more uncluttered the better. Wouldn't you rather have other people judge you by the content of your character than by the jazzy wallpaper that seemed like a good idea five years ago? I'm not a big fan of 'Zoom posturing'; that's to say the people who create (or curate) a statement background, most often in the form of a bookcase full of classic literature. In its own way, this is no less distracting than the out-of-date wallpaper.

Zoom has many uses – think about this before you connect

Just as in the physical workplace there are numerous different ways of presenting, according to need, so it is with virtual meetings.

The amount of effort required to join in on a team meeting with familiar colleagues and a standard agenda isn't the same as for an important presentation to external clients about a subject you are an authority on. Before you press connect, ask yourself, 'Have I prepared to an appropriate level?'

Zoom does not airbrush you, it highlights your flaws

In all my years of helping develop managers through various leadership programmes, I always tried to avoid the topic of 'how to look'. Your dress, your hair, your spectacles, none of these superficial things should matter if you are authoritative, competent and confident. But they do. We know from hard-won experience that judgements are made the very second we walk into that interview room, and the same is true when we pop up on other people's screens for the first time.

As my mother once said to me, 'You look like the wreck of the Hesperus'; I wasn't quite sure what it meant, but I went and tidied myself up. If you put on make-up or have a shave for a day at the office, so should you for a Zoom call. However you dress for the old way of work, that's what you need to wear now.

Countless trainees have told me how much they hate the way they sound when hearing their recorded voice back and I just tell them to 'let it go'. The same rule applies if you don't like the version of you that's on your screen. Simply make the effort to make the very best of yourself, then focus on the other attendees.

Zoom demands your attention (and wears you out)

It's laughable when you think back to the point where we all realized that Zoom would replace many face-to-face, office-based meetings, thinking that we'd have the life of Riley, sitting at home, jumping on to a meeting when needed. Little did we realize just how tiring this way of working could be.

Try to take account of this and limit your own Zoom time, with scheduled breaks in between, otherwise your 'presentation' to others is likely to suffer. Also remember that whoever else is on your call will have the same potential for 'Zoom fatigue', so try to make allowances for this too.

Even if you only managed to secure the role of 'third spear-carrier' in the school play, at every moment you were on stage, there was at least one member of the audience focused on you, rather than what the lead actors were doing. Remember that. If you think that stifled yawn 40 minutes into your Zoom call won't be noticed because someone else is 'holding forth' at the time, then you're wrong.

Top Zoom tips

Package your content

Over the years I have learned a massive amount from my friend and co-author, Professor Cary Cooper, who, as well as having an esteemed career as an academic, has also been the 'expert of choice' for many broadcasters over the years, especially when it comes to workplace stress.

One of the reasons he is so often contacted is that he has a gift for 'packaging' his answers, which is exactly what the media demands. They don't have time for someone who rambles on; their listeners' attention spans won't run to heavy and detailed argument. Just answer this, what's your point, why does it matter, what next? These are exactly the skills needed for Zoom. Get in, get on, get out.

Positive set-up language is also part of the package. You'll often hear an experienced 'expert' preface the point they're about to make with 'What's fascinating about this study', or 'I was amazed to discover', where else do you think click bait stole it's 'teasers' from? I hope the very mention of that signals you need to be sparing in your use of these 'intros'; if you keep hammering home just how fascinated you are, by fairly mundane things, you will very soon be discovered. It's just one more tool to use, when the time is right.

Master the art of the Zoom chairperson

You will know by now that effective presentation is not about shouting louder or longer than anyone else. It's much more to do with well-honed content, delivered in an authentic and sincere way. It is also very much the case that you will make more of an impact if you are able to stay in control and a good way to achieve this is by volunteering to chair the meeting.

Common sense and an understanding of the culture you work in will guide you here, especially when thinking about what an appropriate level of formality will fit (do your meetings have regimented minutes, or just some bullet point notes that you circulate afterwards, for example?).

Set some rules, but be inclusive. What I mean here is, don't read the riot act at the start of the call, but instead deliver a pre-prepared speech (it's a presentation in itself actually) about how you want to get the best out of the call. Below is an example you can adapt:

Good afternoon everyone and thanks for joining us. I'm just going to kick things off by running through what we're trying to achieve today and share some ideas about how we can best go about that.

Hopefully by the time we finish, we'll have come to some sort of consensus about (TOPIC IN HAND) and so I'm encouraging all of you to participate and put your point of view. For everyone's sake, I've tried to summarize my views so that we keep on track time-wise, and if possible I'd like you to do the same.

So, if everyone's in agreement, I suggest we get started, and I'll ask you to speak in the following order, after which

I'll throw things open for a more unstructured discussion (OUTLINE THE RUNNING ORDER).

Shut up and listen!

As well as being the title of my first book, 'Shut up and Listen' is also great advice for Zoom meetings, even more so than when you're face to face. It's obvious that if everyone talks at once, no one can hear anything and there is something about the dynamic of the physical presence of another person that signals to us that they're about to speak, or haven't finished what they were going to say; that same dynamic is absent on Zoom, so you need to keep your eyes peeled for signals.

A cacophony of voices is also a very hard listen, as you try to pick out who is saying what; too much of this feeds into the fatigue I mentioned earlier.

Keep important 'assets' to hand

There's a long-standing joke that newsreaders are just wearing jogging bottoms under the desk, but because all we can see is their top half, they get away with it. As an aside, when Zoom first burst onto the scene with the advent of more people working from home, sales of smart 'top half' clothing soared.

However, the point I'm trying to make here is that your 'audience' can't see everything at your end, so keep important, relevant documents close at hand and, if necessary, make some bulleted lists before you go online, to refer to during the presentation.

You can look extra slick by taping this to the wall directly behind the position of your laptop's camera, effectively creating your own 'autocue'. You can appear to be 'looking down the barrel of the lens' while reading your pre-prepared prompts.

Improvement tips

Getting better at Zoom presentations is exactly the same as when you're delivering face to face. Here's a quick reminder of some of the main points:

- Prepare – be proportionate in the time you spend, but don't go into any meeting without having taken a few minutes at least to familiarize yourself with the purpose of it, the people involved, and the expectations they have of you. Make a note of what you want out of it too.

- Rule of three – it's more important than ever to keep your content 'tight', so if you're outlining an argument, keep your rationale down to three main points and deliver them succinctly.

- Rehearse – do this 'out loud' as that's when your best editing will come. When you hear what you're *actually* going to say, you are then best placed to decide if it works or not.

- Deliver – just like a 'live' presentation with an audience, remember to 'project' a little; this will add weight to your content and make you look more believable.

- Review – you may need to ask permission to record the session, but the tools are there to do it, so you have a great opportunity to not only critique your own performance, but to learn from others' mistakes or technique.

Activity

Use the camera in your device to record yourself delivering a short presentation on a topic of your choice. As well as thinking about how the content comes across, consider how you look and sound. Are you authentic and believable? If possible, review your presentation with a trusted colleague and ask for their feedback.

Summary points

- Don't take Zoom meetings casually; they're an opportunity to make an impression.
- Zoom can be very unforgiving; it highlights your flaws and exaggerates your mistakes.
- Prepare for a Zoom session as you would for any other meeting or presentation.
- Listen (attentively) much more than you speak.
- Take time to review your Zoom technique and set your own improvement goals.

08
Rehearsal

I am not saying that the writing part is easy, but great presentations are really made in the rehearsal phase. The converse applies; if you don't prepare enough, you can never expect to be a polished performer – it's that simple. Time then to move on and look at how you take your well-crafted words from the flatness of the printed page and, through trial and error, breathe life into them, as a finished presentation.

But how, when, where and what amount of rehearsal is needed? This chapter is here to guide you and answer these questions.

Back in Chapter 2 we looked at keeping a 'sense of proportion' by asking: What is this presentation for? Who is it going to be delivered to? What is riding on it? When you have answered those questions you can start to form a mind's-eye picture of you performing. Will you be wandering the stage, unfettered by notes or slides, passionately delivering a seamless speech you have learned word for word? Or is it sufficient, under the circumstances, to stand behind a lectern with a script in front of you and a carefully worked-out PowerPoint presentation?

Keeping things in perspective and deciding on your delivery method will drive all your ongoing rehearsals, because they will determine how you wish to appear to your audience. Here are some options:

- You might seem unscripted and brilliantly spontaneous.
- You might make occasional reference to notes or slides.
- You might rely heavily on scripted content.

Depending on the length of your address, it is possible to mix and match some of these elements to produce a really excellent finished speech. If you have learned five minutes of impassioned content as a slam-bang opening and are able to kick off with this, you can then turn to some form of notes and your audience will happily forgive you. Make sure you link the two sections, so you don't look as if you have just lost your thread. Finish the rallying cry with 'So, that's what's before us, these are the challenges we face and if you think it looks tough, it is. Let's take a few minutes to examine what we can do together to make this next year a success.' Then move to the lectern, to continue, with PowerPoint or your written notes.

When it comes to rehearsal, the mistake lots of rookie presenters make is they have the general outline of their speech, so they think it will just all come good on the day. It may be they have structured this with PowerPoint, have written copious notes or have jotted some bullet points on a sheet of A4 – not good enough!

Rehearsal technique

Out loud

The only way to know if your presentation is going to hang together, when you deliver it out loud, is to deliver it… out loud. Not muttered under your breath, but standing up and spoken, in circumstances as near to how the real thing will be as possible.

Tip

How we write and how we speak are two different things. That's why writing authentic dialogue is so difficult. Out loud rehearsal takes your speech from written to spoken language.

This type of rehearsal often influences the final speech in a dramatic way. Once you start to hear back what you've written, it is surprising how many times you think 'No, that just doesn't work' and your self-editing process begins.

If your speech contains a joke (be careful – see Chapter 6) or some storytelling, this is a reminder you really need to become so familiar with it that it flows in a seamless way. If either of these are badly delivered – for example: 'Oh no! Hang on, was it the manager who said "Don't you know who I am?"'... Or was it the CEO?' – you will be much worse off than if you had not bothered telling the joke or story at all.

Tip

You might choose to rehearse out loud, in front of a trusted colleague or family member, so you can get some feedback. This is often more nerve-racking than standing up in a room full of strangers, but it is a good way to improve your performance.

Duration

There are two important things to say about the length of your speech. The first is it should be however long you have promised; the second is it should be paced. Let's look at each aspect separately.

Really slick, professional presenters don't go over their allocated time, nor do they come up short. There are a number of good reasons why they are able to do this. Through hard-won experience and practice, they may have an off-the-shelf presentation they have delivered many times before and so know it fits a particular time span. Alternatively, by having written and delivered presentations over a number of years, they have got used to interpreting the amount of written material they have into a time frame. As a rule of thumb, a typed page of A4 takes around three minutes to read aloud.

Another good way of assessing the spoken length of a speech is to divide the word count by three, which will give you the number of seconds (the formula used in broadcast television is that we speak at three words per second), then divide by 60 and you'll have the number of minutes. Word processing software will display the word count for you as your starting point. This method is surprisingly accurate.

Pacing

If you are a little less experienced and are delivering a completely new presentation, then this concept of pacing is critical. It is done by developing a modular presentation, with primary and secondary messages, that can be 'flexed' as you go along. This means having a core set of points with supplementary content, for example a selection of illustrative stories, that can lengthen the speech if you are coming up short or be dropped altogether if time is running out.

A word of warning

Be careful not to have too many slides in your presentation if you need to be flexible with your delivery. There is nothing worse than being 20 minutes into a half-hour presentation knowing that you have only covered 5 per cent of your slides. Audiences get a bit restless if you say, 'We'll skip the next dozen slides', as they wonder what they are missing and you look ill-prepared.

Modular presentations work best with fewer slides that can either be 'talked up' or briefly described, according to how your timings are going; then only you will know what you have skipped or lengthened.

You may think that it seems like quite an advanced technique to rewrite the script in your head as you go – and it is. However, it becomes easier, surprisingly quickly, when you deliver lots of presentations.

The really clever bit is to do it without members of the audience noticing (see the box 'A word of warning' above). You don't want them to feel short-changed by not getting everything you have prepared or to think you such an amateur that you have got the timings badly wrong.

A good trick is to have a presentation with a number of 'break points' in it as this will give you the breathing space to make adjustments to the length of your spoken content. This might be as simple as showing a video clip. Then while the audience are watching, you can check where you are up to, assess how much content you have left and make some instant editing decisions if necessary. Alternatively, you might set the audience a simple task, like thinking of three things that inspirational leaders do. While they are busy, you can do a bit of rejigging.

The final important thing to say about pacing is that you have to consider your entire piece in terms of the pace it is delivered. It is fine to add a bit of drama by having a slam-bang opening or a rousing finish delivered at a punchier pace than the rest of the talk, but, overall, you need to aim to keep it even. Suddenly rushing through the last six slides will alert your audience to the fact that you have messed up the timing and are trying to shoehorn too much into a short time frame.

Time it

It makes sense that you will only know how long your presentation is if you time it. During rehearsal, use a stopwatch to get an accurate picture of how long you are speaking for. If you stop to make notes or amend your presentation while you are rehearsing, don't forget to pause the clock too.

When it comes to 'real life', you will find many presentation suites have a clock at the back of the room, so the speaker can check the time. If not, take your wristwatch off before you start and prop it up on the lectern, so that you can keep track of the time without the audience knowing.

Recital

How well should you know your presentation? The answer is based on a number of factors. To help you decide, consider the following:

- How long is the total speech?
- How often will you have to deliver it?
- How do you want to be perceived?
- What are the expectations of the audience?
- How easily do you memorize?

The older we get, the harder it is to commit things to memory, so be more selective about what you choose to put in your speech. That said, if you are going to deliver the same speech time and again, make the effort to memorize as much of it as possible.

Later, we'll look in detail at the importance of the start and end of your presentations, but for now I would like to emphasize that it is worth the effort to try and get these sections 'off pat', especially the opening, as this will help to settle your nerves.

Stories and anecdotes are also quite easy to remember (which is why we use them on our audiences), or if you have constructed a presentation around three key points, you should be able to recall them easily enough. However, if you want to learn to remember material more easily, are there any helpful ways of going about it?

Memory tips

- Turn the entire presentation into a story in your head. If there is narrative flow, you will remember what's coming next much more easily. When you are at the writing stage, make sure the sequence of steps is logical, leading towards a moral at the end.

- Use alliteration on your main points. For example, you could talk about the 'three Rs' as personal attributes of managers: resilience, resourcefulness and reflection. The points are much easier to remember in that format.

- Divide up your script and learn it in bite-size pieces. Try to master one section completely before moving on to the next. As already mentioned, learn the start and end sections before anything else.

- Record and play back. Commit your speech to a recorded format. When you listen back in the car, on your commuter journey or when cooking dinner, try to anticipate the next bit before it arrives.

- Stand and deliver. When you have a reasonable working knowledge of the presentation, try a dummy run, making quick mental notes of the bits you struggled over. Pretend it is a real-life scenario and go from start to finish as best you can, before reviewing the sections you know less well.

On the subject of rehearsal, let's close by posing a question. Can you rehearse too much?

I don't really think you can. The better you know your material, the more scope there is to put some real meaning into it. If it is a constant struggle to recall the next thing you are going to say, you haven't got much brain capacity left for thinking about how well you are delivering.

Striding around the office, or at home, reciting your latest speech might make you feel daft, but compare this to how stupid you could end up looking if you forget during a presentation what you were going to say. If that doesn't make you uncomfortable enough to take rehearsal seriously, nothing will.

Activity

Write and memorize a three-sentence generic opening to a speech. This could include something about the venue (regardless of where it is), a few words about yourself and/or the reasons why you are delighted to be making this presentation. Make sure you can deliver this opening without hesitation.

Summary points

- Begin by deciding how much of the presentation you are going to commit to memory. This will drive your rehearsal schedule.

- At the very least, learn your opening and closing lines, so you have a strong start and finish.

- There is no replacement for rehearsing out loud; only then can you get a real sense of how you will sound on the day.

- Concentrate on keeping an even pace throughout the speech and reflect afterwards on how well this worked. What could you do better next time?

- Use the memory tips in this chapter or find your own ways of learning material off pat.

09
Finding your voice

So far, the brief has been set (either by someone else or to your own agenda), you have written the content, added some interesting stories and rehearsed until you feel ready to hit the stage. Next we come to the actual delivery of your speech, a key part of which is the sound of your voice.

We hear our voice partly through our ears but also by the sound waves travelling through our skull, owing to a thing called bone conductivity. This is why when we listen to a recording of ourselves, it comes as a shock and the more we protest to those around us that it doesn't sound anything like our voice, the more they assure us it does. So, the best thing is to get used to it.

In extreme cases, people have set about changing their voice radically. One such example was British Prime Minister Margaret Thatcher, who in the 1970s was coached by a television producer to lower the tone of her strident voice by 46 hertz, to give depth and authority to it. If you too are thinking of running for office, then please feel free to take the same route; otherwise, stick with what you have got, with a few minor tweaks (see below).

Regional accents are fine, as long as they are not so broad that anyone from outside your town would struggle to understand you.

Consider the following four aspects of voice, power, pitch, passion and pace.

Power

How loud or soft our normal speaking voice is doesn't really matter. If we remember to 'project' a little more on stage it has the effect of appearing confident, but in a larger room, where microphones may well be used, a quieter voice can be amplified.

Sometimes it's more important to remember to vary the power, rather than have everything at the same volume; this makes the speech more dramatic.

Pitch

When it comes to the rise and fall in our voices, how high or low they are, the same applies as with 'power': there needs to be a bit of variation. Failing to do so will leave you delivering in a dull monotone, guaranteed to send your audience to sleep. Don't over exaggerate this, but try to be conscious of using some 'light and shade'. Incidentally, remembering to do this is much easier if you're very familiar with your content, through rigorous rehearsal.

Passion

Show some emotion. You can do this through your voice. The rise and fall we have just examined will happen much more naturally if there are parts of your presentation you feel really strongly about. Pause a moment and think about the difference in your delivery if you were presenting the company's annual results, as opposed to speaking on behalf of a charitable foundation that you support. Now, inside your head, try to hear the difference in your voice.

Pace

Slow down! That is the general rule for the infrequent speech maker. It does require some degree of concentration, as there is a physiological reason we go too fast, especially at the start. Our natural 'fight or flight' response has been triggered and we have gallons of adrenaline pumping through our system – no wonder we go at it like an express train. The plain truth is, we just want to get it over with and sit down again.

Umms and errs

I have no idea why it is, but it seems to be getting harder to avoid the tons of 'verbal garbage' that chokes what we are trying to say in an articulate way. I have to try really hard to eliminate the 'umms' and the 'errs' – and when it comes to the 'y'knows', even more concentration is required.

Good idea

So far there have been a couple of nods to what I call 'stage persona'. This is the character the audience sees and will most likely rely on a particular aspect of who we are off-stage. It's worth reflecting now and then on how your audience sees you; if you're happy with the 'character', keep playing it that way.

It takes most people a while to work out who that person is, so don't rush the process. When you hear professional performers interviewed, they'll quite often say that it took them a while to find the voice that's the authentic version of them.

We finish this chapter by looking at the work of Albert Mehrabian from the University of California, back in the 1960s. The Mehrabian study (Figure 9.1) looked at a range of factors that might influence

Figure 9.1   Mehrabian study

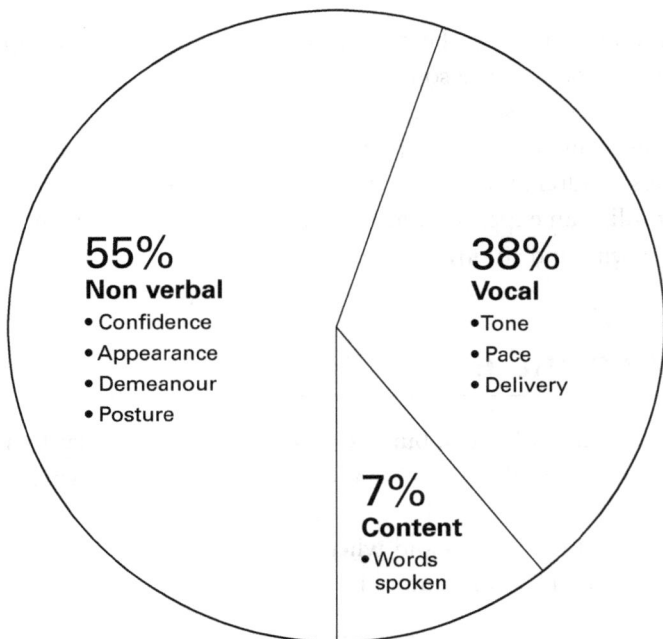

an audience's ability to become engaged and interested in a speaker. Over half (55 per cent) of the impact of a performance came from non-verbal factors, such as confidence, appearance, demeanour and posture, so think hard about these when you are reading the relevant sections in this book. Of the rest of the factors, 38 per cent fell into a category that could broadly be called 'vocal' – tone, pace, etc (see above). You may have worked this out – that leaves only 7 per cent of influence from the *actual words spoken*. So this is important stuff, but don't lose focus, you still have to deliver the words!

Activity

Record your voice in a variety of circumstances and settings and listen back to it. Balance up the more informal, social situations with some more focused business scenarios, including when you are presenting. Go beyond the first response of not liking the sound of your voice and try to review the recordings objectively, so you can improve your vocal projection.

Summary points

- Use your own voice. Don't try to copy or mimic another accent or the delivery of a different speaker. Make the best of who you are.

- Be prepared to speak out, loud and clear. Varying the power of your voice will help to maintain audience interest.

- Avoid the pitfalls of pace. Make a conscious effort to slow down in order to articulate your words properly. It will make you look more confident too.

- Stay conscious about the sound of your voice and what you are saying, so that you can try and vocalize seamlessly.

10
Openings

Although the importance of opening your speech strongly has already been mentioned, we haven't yet covered the best way of doing this. This chapter looks at the 'hows' and 'whys' of openings.

Good idea

Before you think about stepping up to the podium there is a prior stage of preparation, which is to think about how you would like to be introduced. What your host says to welcome you to the stage will begin to influence the audience, so if you want to stay in control of this, you will need to write your own introduction, keeping it short – and witty, if possible – or brief the person who is introducing you on what to say. This will make life much easier as you start your speech.

From a structural point of view, the opening of your presentation is, without doubt, the most important part. The reason the first few sentences you say are so critical is that they have a huge influence on everyone in the room: members of the audience and, just as importantly, you the presenter.

How you start is who you are; your audience will make up their minds instantly. As you want the rest of this performance to go well, it is critical that you get them on your side, right at the top. Although engaging people is really important, making sure you don't disengage them in the first few minutes is even more vital.

Lots of speakers do this, simply by not having a strong, positive enough opening.

Tip
Never, never, never

Never begin a presentation with an apology. Whatever might have gone wrong, you need to open with a positive comment, before acknowledging the broken air conditioning, the failure of the PowerPoint or the lack of natural daylight.

False starts

In many presentation situations there is a minefield of 'false starts' to be navigated. Distractions can get in the way of launching off in a positive way. Some of these are foisted upon us by others, such as where the organizer asks if you will announce where the toilets are and the fact that no fire alarm is expected today. This kind of 'statutory requirement' may be unavoidable, for the sake of health, safety and comfort, but avoid making it the first thing you say. Get your 'big opening' out of the way first, then backtrack to this sort of dull information.

Surprisingly, many of the false starts you hear are nothing to do with the organizers, but down solely to the haplessness of the presenters themselves. How many times have you witnessed an opening like these?

'Hello, can you hear me at the back?'

'There are still a few more stragglers to come, but I think we'll get started.'

'Did everyone get a pack with the slides in it when they arrived?'

These are not openings, they are disasters. Professional presenters don't get distracted by worrying whether their audience can hear them; they have already sound checked the room in advance. The same applies to the other examples; they are just audio wallpaper, contributing nothing useful and getting in the way, spoiling what could otherwise have been a great opening.

These are all classed as 'false' starts, because members of the audience were hoping to hear a powerful introduction to whatever the presenter was going to talk about, not some trivia that doesn't affect them or that can be dealt with in another way.

Don't let distractions derail your opening. This is most likely to happen because of latecomers, but remember it is *their* fault they are late, not yours. You have no obligation to make them feel at ease for sneaking in after everyone else. In fact, if you do, you are sending out a signal that says, 'Hey, it's OK to turn up late, it's only me you've come to listen to.'

My advice is that you ensure in advance that the entry door will not break your line of sight with the audience, so that latecomers are not forced to walk across you to get to a seat. Instead, make sure the room is configured so the stage is at the opposite end to the entrance.

The next thing you do is completely ignore the latecomers. This does two things. First, it says you are in control, and second, it marginalizes them, rather than glorifying their entrance. If you are running a full-day conference and you are the main speaker throughout the event, it is much less likely that people will return late from the breaks if you adopt this behaviour.

The negative start

False starts are bad, negative ones even worse. If you begin on the back foot, why on earth would your audience want to stay and listen? Again, examples to make you cringe are listed below and in case you think that I have made them up, I haven't: they are all real.

'Errrm... I'm not very good at this sort of thing...'

'This next section is a bit boring, but...'

'I'm not sure why they've asked me to speak...' (Hey there, if you're not sure, how the heck do you think we, as your audience, feel?)

Audiences can find a dozen reasons to dislike you, based on your clothes, hairstyle, voice, demeanour, etc. Don't give them one more!

Table 10.1 Seven deadly sins – how not to open

Sin	Effect on audience
1. Nervous	Audience lose confidence from the off
2. Negative	You've given yourself a mountain to climb
3. Vague	The antithesis of good signposting
4. Apologetic	Lacks the positivity you'd like to engender
5. Uncertain	Appears you are not in control
6. Uninspiring	They'll be preparing themselves for being bored!
7. Stumbling	Signals your lack of preparation and professionalism

Top tips for brilliant beginnings

The kiss of death will befall your presentation if you start with a dull monotone voice, if your opening slide fails to capture the imagination of your audience or if you don't give them any good reason to listen to you – but enough of the negatives, how do you wow your audience from the word go?

Set the right tone

From the very second you stand up to speak, your audience will begin to make a snap judgement about what the next half hour is going to be like. Whatever you decide to say as your opening line, the really important part is to look like you are in control. There's nothing that unnerves an audience more than a presenter who looks unsure.

Good idea

It's sometimes OK to sit on the fence, but there are times when it helps to have an opinion. If you get asked to speak on a hot topic, you'll engage your audience better if you have a firm point of view. Nothing makes people sit up and listen more than a speaker who shows belief (either in favour, or as a detractor). This also makes for a great opening as you firmly nail your colours to the mast. Make sure you have the arguments to back up your case, whatever stance you have taken.

Make 'em laugh

Having a witty opening line is a great way of getting the audience on your side and, just as importantly, helping to relax those tensed-up nerves. There is a distinct difference here between a joke and a witty observation. I have cautioned against joke telling already in case it doesn't get a laugh. If that happens at this early stage in proceedings, it will increase your nervousness.

Witty observation is less risky and often funnier. The state of the economy, a big news story or the nature of your competitors can all be worked upon for a witty one-liner.

A massive step up the scale of brilliant presenters can be taken if you are able to tailor your wit in a topical way. If a universal truth about the lunch you have all just eaten, or the room you are in or the journey to get to the venue occurs to you, then this will really impress your audience.

Tell it straight

There are some circumstances where it is better to leave the comedian back in the dressing room and present in a much more matter-of-fact way. If that is the case, you might decide it is best to 'cut to the chase' right away and simply tell it straight. We saw earlier, when talking about use of humour, that it can be a risky business, so if there's a lot at stake, weigh it up and decide if the risk is worth it.

An example might be as follows: 'In the next 20 minutes, I'm going to do everything possible to convince you that choosing us will secure a long-term, credible, cost-effective supplier relationship that will help to underpin your own business success.' Sometimes, straight is good.

Be complimentary (but not fawning)

If you really are happy to be in Harpenden, or delighted to be in Denver, then it's fine to say so, but you need to be genuine in your sentiment, or the members of the audience will think you are just spinning them a line.

A bit of forethought or research might help you here. Showing you have taken the time to find out about the urban regeneration scheme for the city you are in, or the success of the local sports team, will carry some weight. What is better is if you have a personal anecdote of time spent in the place, for example: 'The last time I was here, my hosts were so hospitable I can't really remember much about the visit. That's why I've had to come back!'

If you can't find a connection, then a contrast can be just as good. Think about where you live, or were born or brought up. Can you reference this by talking about town versus city? Insular versus cosmopolitan? Even European versus US culture? These differences can be a real source of interest.

However you choose to open, keep it snappy. You don't want to lose your way right at the top, or give your audience the impression you may have done so. This tends to rule out long anecdotes or descriptions.

Be absolutely cast-iron sure of the first words that are going to come out of your mouth. Don't rely on 'busking' it – don't ever think, 'I'll start with something about the awful weather we've been having'. Hit them with your first line, rehearsed and rehearsed and perfected, square between the eyes.

Tip

It's not all about me… me… me!

I used to feel so unbelievably flattered if I was asked to speak at an event that I thought it a good idea to justify my presence to the audience, as if I couldn't really believe it myself. On more than one occasion I started with a mini-résumé of my career and what made me suitable to stand before the audience. I think this was a big mistake, not because I now believe I am so brilliant that I need no introduction or justification, it's only that I should be able to prove my worth, my suitability to the event, through what I say and how I say it.

The other thing that happens when you launch off on a long list of 'me, me, me' stories, is you come across as a bit of a big head. Humility is a much more endearing trait; it's better to be a bit humble.

Activity

Write an opening for the next speech you have to deliver or, if necessary, an imaginary one. Read it out loud and think about how it sounds from your point of view. Now, read it again and try to consider objectively what impression it would make on you if you were a member of the audience. This is a good way of testing your opening lines.

Summary points

- Avoid the negative. At the start, stay in control by making a positive statement that asserts who you are.

- Ignore any distractions, especially latecomers. Start on time and don't be put off if anyone enters the room after you have begun.

- Be relevant and appropriate. Think about the needs and wants of the people in your audience; the more topical you are, the easier it will be to engage them.

- Say something nice. Be complimentary to your hosts, or about the venue, town or city you are in.

- Rehearse your opening few lines, so you can deliver them unscripted and with confidence.

11
Endings

For now, let's not worry about all that important content in the middle of your presentation. Let's just fast forward to the end and think about how to get off.

In many ways, endings can be more difficult than openings, often because there is an element of uncertainty over what will happen next. Will you take questions? Is the audience expected to burst into spontaneous applause, or will the host take to the stage to bring on the next speaker? There are so many variables that it is up to you to grip the thing by the throat and have it done your way. Let's begin by dealing with how you finish.

Make the ending definite

Don't fizzle out into nothingness. After all the hard work you've put in, you deserve to have a memorable ending that has lasting impact. I have heard speakers who have said:

'Well, that's about it really...'

'There's more stuff in the notes if you want to read up later...'

'I think I'm probably out of time, so I'd better stop...'

Your end sentence should be written and rehearsed just as rigorously as your opening. It should be powerful, it should leave no doubt that you've finished, and it should most probably end 'Thank you.'

Make it upbeat

Maybe I am stating the obvious when I say finish on a high, but you would be amazed at the number of presentations that don't. In many cases, this is because speakers simply haven't thought of having an upbeat ending. They may round things off nicely with a comprehensive summary of what they have said and finish by thanking their audience for listening, but it is hardly inspiring stuff.

Optimism is the key here. Whatever you have presented, even if the content has been doom and gloom laden, you have to leave your audience believing things will be better tomorrow; there is a bright new horizon and the future is filled with exciting opportunities. Often, it is in the face of adversity that great orators emerge. I think this is related to their ability to make the audience believe things can only get better.

Make it tight

From a structural point of view, think about how the last five minutes of the presentation are going to go. The summary will be pretty familiar territory to you. Most of us summarize as a matter of course. You also need to clear the decks of 'parish notices' as they are sometimes called, for example what happens next? When will the coffee break be? Is there going to be a question and answer session? You may even need to introduce the next speaker. All these 'domestic' issues might be important to the smooth running of the event, but they make rubbish endings to your presentation. Get them out of the way before your big finish.

Leave yourself a minute right at the end, to deliver your well-written, carefully rehearsed, tightly packaged finale. Build towards it and at the appropriate moment, stop. Your applause will follow. A good lead in to these last few sentences might be as follows:

'I've talked about some serious issues today; we have, without doubt, some exceptionally difficult challenges to meet; but I'd like you to remember this...'

Or alternatively:

'Out of everything I've said today, there is one thing that stands out for me as more important than anything, and that is...'

Make it passionate

As we have outlined, passion – really caring about something – is one of the key ingredients great speakers harness.

It's fine to let your feelings shine through during the course of your presentation, but I would say it is *essential* to give them full rein as you reach the end. Speak from the heart and your audience are bound to warm to you as a person.

A footnote to all this is that 'passion' does not always entail shouting. Passion can be quiet, it can be determined, it can be as much the look in your eye as the tone in your voice. If you really mean it, you don't need to worry about how this will come across, your natural feelings will carry you through.

Below, I've outlined a typical running order to finish a presentation.

Outro

1 Manage expectations: 'This has been a complex issue and I'm happy to take some questions in our run-up to coffee break at 11 o'clock, but before that I want to finish by reiterating one important point...'

2 Passionate ending – call to action, rallying cry, plea for support.

3 Bang! You shut up.

4 Applause (rapturous, obviously).

5 Question and answer session.

6 Round off the question and answer session with a final rallying cry.

7 Coffee.

Applause

I have attended hundreds of 'fizzle-out' presentations, where not even the merest ripple of applause has broken out at the end. Applause is important for a couple of reasons. Firstly, you have worked hard to write, rehearse and deliver this presentation. You deserve some reward for it and an appreciative audience is usually enough payback for most of us.

Secondly, and this is the vital bit, applause makes the audience feel better. They are sharing with their fellow delegates in a positive feeling, brought about by what you have just told them. Why wouldn't they want to break out into spontaneous clapping?

A quick final note about national culture. It is not too much of a stereotype to suggest that Brits are more reserved than their US or Australian counterparts. Remember that the territory you are in might have an effect on the readiness to applaud!

Figure 11.1 shows a few things to consider when developing your ending.

Figure 11.1 Endings mind map

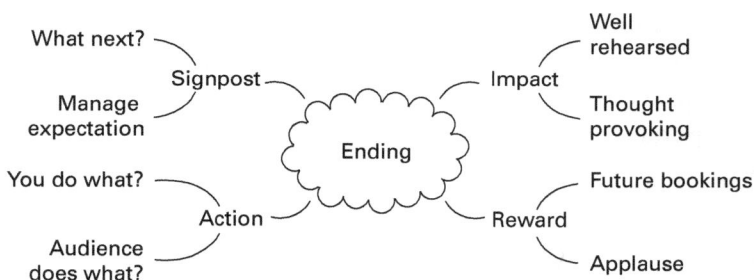

Activity

Complete the following phrase: 'My passion is…' Now, write a 100-word piece that would serve as an ending to a speech on this topic. Read it back, then edit it down to just 50 words. This should give you a powerful ending.

Summary points

- Never fizzle out! Make your ending purposeful and definite and leave your audience in no doubt you have finished.

- The last thing you say is what your audience will remember the most. Choose the single, most important point from your presentation to finish on.

- A good, strong ending keeps the control with you. It will help to make you look assertive and confident.

- Audiences like to know what's going on. With a well-planned ending, you can manage their expectations.

- The applause resulting from a strong ending leaves a positive feeling in the room.

12
Handling your nerves

When I'm teaching a group about presentation skills, the 'fear' which is most often voiced is that they will be nervous. I could just say 'it's part of the territory, get on with it', but there are things we can do to help manage our nerves. Before I begin that process though, it's time for a confession. 'Presenting' is pretty much what I've done for a living most of my working life. I still get nervous. I long ago gave up on expecting the feeling to disappear completely. Instead I now accept it and do all I can to manage it.

So, the strategies I've outlined here won't make your nervousness go away, but, over time, will help you stay in control of it.

Rationalize

Let's start with the toughest one. We can probably agree that some 'fears' are not a hostage to logic; but just because we find them hard to explain, it doesn't mean the feelings aren't real. I think it's a good strategy to find some quiet time in advance of an upcoming presentation and to really think through 'what am I afraid of?'

In another context, I met an international aid worker, who spent her life in disaster zones, the sort of places that would scare most of us. I asked if she felt trepidation and she replied, 'I just think, what's the worst that could happen, and then I get on with it.' Like me, you may feel 'easier said than done', but by taking this approach we can, with practice, begin to put our own misgivings in context.

A very common fear is that something will go wrong, so here is a strategy to combat this.

Control

Not many of us would consider 'control freak' as a particularly complimentary label, but when it comes to presenting, it really is a good thing. Elsewhere in the text, I talk about the need to prepare properly and there are several checklists, covering behaviour and equipment for you to use. I don't suggest that by covering all the bases your confidence will increase, but by *not* doing so, we run the risk of having it severely dented at a time when it matters most.

On the day of a presentation, we want to have our best opportunity of performing well. Get the logistics sorted in advance and you'll be doing yourself a favour – all your focus will be on you and what you're going to say.

Understand

Be realistic about the 'jitters'. Standing in front of an audience can leave us feeling exposed. Potentially we could make a fool of ourselves and that is what drives much of our nervousness. Now contextualize those feelings. How often have you seen a disaster happen? (And if you did, what was the reason?) This should help you come to terms with the rising feeling of panic many of us feel.

Build confidence

There's more on this topic later in the book, but for now let me say that confidence is something we can nurture and build. Take control of the public speaking part of your career and find opportunities to practise, in safe spaces first (where the audience isn't too large and the subject is well known to you) and incrementally move to the outer edges of your comfort zone. When a presentation has gone well, take time to congratulate yourself and remember these 'wins' next time you get up to speak.

One of the universal truths of being nervous is that these feelings begin to subside once you're in your flow. That is why I'm so keen for you to know your opening; it gets you off to the right start and helps you settle.

The nerves curve in Figure 12.1 shows a typical pattern.

Figure 12.1 The nerves curve

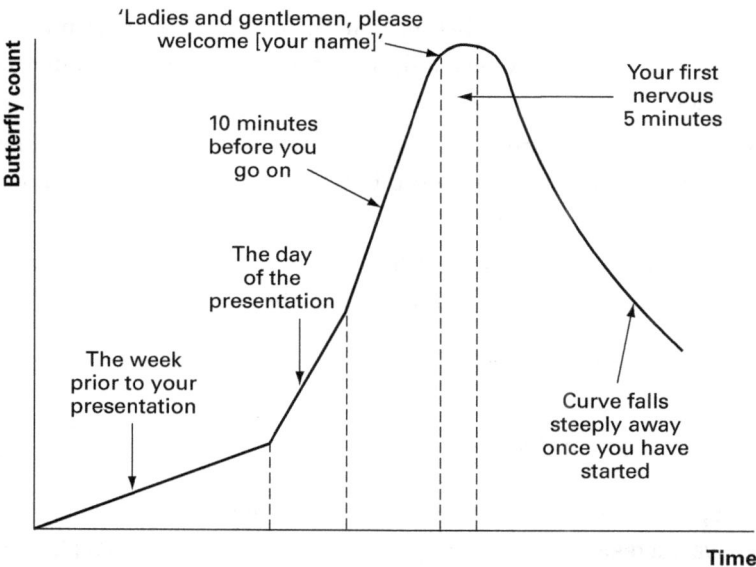

Further tips for helping you manage your nerves are outlined in the checklist below.

Antidote to nerves – checklist

- Prepare – cover all the bases, including the contingency planning.

- Practise – make sure you have mastered your presentation before you arrive. You don't want to be rehearsing right up to the last minute.

- Stay in control – don't let other people's lack of preparation hijack your professionalism. Turn up, be gracious and do what you promised to do.

- Be early – even if you have to sit in the car park for half an hour. Better that than rushing in, hot and flustered, at the last minute.

- Avoid stimulants – don't drink caffeine for an hour before you present, otherwise you may find it will make your heart race. Never drink alcohol before a speech.

- Hydrate – sip water before you get up (to stop your mouth drying) and keep some handy, near the lectern. Be careful not to knock it over!

- Breathe – if you stop doing this, you won't be able to present, or do anything else. Take a deep breath before you start and don't rush.

- Concentrate – get the first few sentences out of the way, then let your nerves start to calm down all by themselves.

Tip
Look them in the eye

Eye contact is an important part of the presenter's toolkit. When we are feeling nervous it might be hard to relax and look people in the eye, but not doing so gives the impression we are shifty and untrustworthy. Try to remember to scan around the room and momentarily meet the eyes of as many members of the audience as possible. It makes them much more engaged with what you are saying.

Body language

In order to avoid looking nervous, many people put too much emphasis on controlling their body language in pressurized situations. I am not dismissive of the concept that how we are feeling inside is 'leaked' out to people around us, by the unconscious posture, actions and mannerisms we display; however, there is not a lot that we can do to address it at a conscious level.

Let me give you an example from real life. You may have been in a high-pressure situation in the past, such as a job interview, when you have suddenly become conscious of your body language. You are sitting there, with your legs so tightly crossed they have wound around each other like a jungle creeper. Your upper body is bunched and tense and your arms are folded tightly across your chest. You simply couldn't look less relaxed. Suddenly you remember all about body language and uncurl yourself, to sit in an open, pseudo-relaxed mode. Two minutes later, you have forgotten again and are back to being almost foetal.

The point is, if you are going to get your body language right, it is much better to deal with the root cause, which is your underlying tension. Genuinely find ways of relaxing and your body will follow. Simply reminding yourself to alter what is your 'natural state' will only result in you reverting to it all too quickly.

And a final word, because we can get a bit twitchy and nervous when on stage we do have a tendency to fidget more than usual, so take any loose change or keys out of your pockets, so you don't start 'jangling'. Only carry in your hand what is necessary, such as your cue cards or script.

Face up to the fact that being nervous is an emotional reaction. For most of us it will always be there and you can take heart that most professional speakers think it is a good thing. When you stop being nervous is when you start getting complacent.

Activity

Before your next presentation, make a disaster checklist. On a sheet of paper, write down everything that could feasibly go wrong that would prevent you from being your best. With each item on the list, consider what action you can take now to mitigate the risk.

Summary points

- Being nervous is natural. Don't be surprised or disturbed about it, every good speaker feels the same at some point.
- Confidence is the antidote to the jitters, so look for every available opportunity to build it.
- Prepare properly and you will minimize the risk of things going wrong, thereby reducing your worries.
- Let your body language take care of itself. Too much effort concentrating on this will mean you run the risk of making mistakes with other aspects of your presentation.

13
Handling your audience

We have established that the audience is probably the single, most important factor when considering a new presentation, but what exactly is 'an audience'? How can we get to know it better? How can we be more in tune with it and encourage it to respond positively to what we are saying?

Fear of the audience

If you think that you're the only one who is nervous when you get up to speak, you'd be wrong; the audience is 'in fear' too. Here's why.

Most of us have had the experience of going to a live performance of something we know little about, like a concert or a comedy show. When the curtain goes up the thought at the forefront of our minds is, 'I hope this isn't awful'. That's how your audience will be. Get the opening right and you will have set them at ease from the beginning. Getting it wrong isn't irredeemable, but why give yourself a mountain to climb?

From the off, you want them to feel they're in safe hands; this is going to be OK. That's why I keep banging on about the importance of starting well.

More than simply a collection of individuals, audiences have a group momentum; applause breeds applause, laughter stimulates laughter and so on.

For the sake of argument an audience is in a neutral state before you begin. What happens next is critical. Look at the audience swingometer (Figure 13.1). If you can get them collectively swinging to the right, momentum builds and soon you're flying; to the left and you've got a job on your hands.

Figure 13.1   Audience swingometer

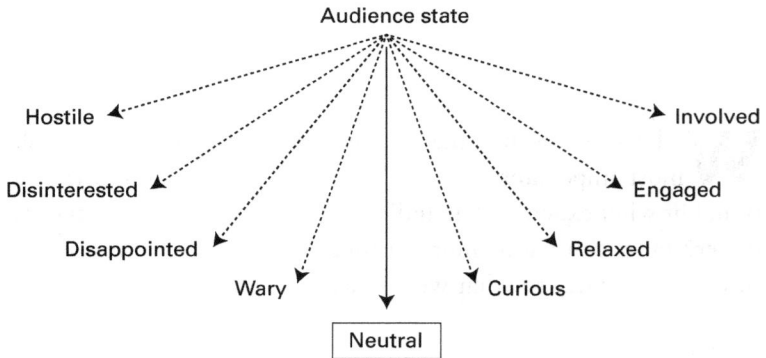

When it comes to openings, try to remember that the audience, in general, is a timid creature. It can be easily frightened, so don't kick off with anything too intimidating – unless it has a specific shock purpose. If you ask a question as an opener, make it a rhetorical one; don't expect an answer! Here is an example:

'Is it just me, or has technology just got too complicated these days...?'

Follow this up quickly with something like:

'That's the question I was asking myself as I sat on hold, waiting for the IT helpdesk to respond.'

Tip

Even a 'neutral' state can vary. Organizational culture, prevailing trading conditions and management style can all have an effect on how this audience is feeling *today*. If you can chat to a few folk on the way in you might be able to gauge the mood; if not, look for other clues. Body language is often a giveaway when it comes to how 'engaged' people are. Try to get used to reading the room.

We know the customer is always right and that applies to your audience too. However they are feeling, it's your job to win them over.

Build your skills

If you decide to interact with your audience, avoid being too adventurous to begin with. Don't get me wrong, it's a great trick if you can pull it off and some of the most successful speakers are the ones who are able to really engage. The difficulty is you never know what you are going to get, so you need to be able to deal with any reaction. Some gentle introductions to audience interaction are listed below, before we look at this aspect in more detail:

- Ask for a show of hands. Make it something simple, so that people don't have to sit and debate the issue. Follow up by saying what the rough percentages are: 'So, it looks to me like about two-thirds of you feel like there aren't enough hours in the day to do your job.'

- Make a teasing statement. As long as the members of the audience know what it is you are doing, they will play along; just be careful not to upset anyone along the way. For example: 'I was speaking to your CEO earlier and he was telling me most of you feel as though you are paid way too much money for the hours you put in.'

- Try gentle humour; for example: 'When I was invited to speak here today and told that I'd be addressing an audience of the most talented personnel managers in the country, I couldn't resist the opportunity. Then, when I arrived, I found there was a double bonus, because you lot turned up as well.'

- Apply rhetorical ambiguity. This is when you ask a question where people feel as though they are probably not supposed to answer, but are not quite sure; for example: 'It's probably only me who feels this way, but I sometimes think we get sent too much e-mail!' Or turn it on its head (which will add some humour): 'I don't know about you, but sometimes I worry that I'm not getting enough e-mail!'

Audience interaction

Selecting a victim

This strategy is not for the faint-hearted. A good practical demonstration, using a member of the audience, can win hearts and minds, but it is extremely risky. Don't ever do anything that will humiliate a member of the audience.

If you are going to do anything physical, you had better make sure in advance that your 'volunteers' are up to it. Choosing someone who is less able will cause embarrassment all round – the kind you are unlikely to recover from.

Finally, let me present you with a balanced view of audience interaction.

The case for

Using a member of the audience can take you closer to the crowd as a whole: if you do it skilfully, other people in the room will warm to you. Getting everyone to join in (perhaps to shout out a word or phrase on cue) is also bound to give a feeling of involvement to all present.

Really good handling of an audience is amusing, engaging and warm. It creates a fantastic atmosphere, makes you likeable and your messages memorable.

The case against

If you try but fail to deliver audience interaction, the results can be devastating. If you ask an open question and no one answers, or call for a volunteer to come up on stage and there isn't a taker, the embarrassment of everyone involved is palpable. Tricks, practical demonstrations or experiments that go wrong will not only fail to illustrate the point you were trying to make, they will actively contradict it. Someone who is uncomfortable with you on stage will make the audience squirm. Someone who is funnier than you will make you look stupid.

The conclusion

Love the members of your audience, but treat them with respect. Over time, think of gentle ways you might get them to join in. Plan these interventions carefully and always have a contingency plan in case they don't work out. Keep your moments of audience interaction as an optional extra. You can try them if things are going well, or wait for another day if the audience is tough.

Activity

For your next presentation, come up with a list of three rhetorical questions you could ask the audience, either as an opener or in the body of the speech as a way of engaging with them. Choose the strongest one and try it out on the day.

Summary points

- There is nothing more important than the people in your audience. Handle them carefully – you need them on your side.

- Although a collection of individuals, audiences often display group behaviours. Winning over one can mean winning over all.

- Audiences have 'momentum'; try to get it moving in the right direction from the off.

- If you decide you want to interact with audiences, begin with something simple and build up over time.

- Always be polite to the members of your audience – you never know when one of them might want to book you again.

14
Question and answer sessions

The thought of a Q&A session, at the end of a speech, strikes fear in the hearts of most people. The first thing to say is this is not always necessary, we've just got into a kind of habit where speakers are expected to do it and audiences are expected to suffer it.

I say 'suffer' because there are so many times when we have to sit and witness a stilted or stage-managed question and answer session. The inevitable outcome of this is when you break for coffee, the thing uppermost in the minds of your audience is not the sparkling address you have just given, but the dull-as-ditchwater inquisition that followed it; not a good way to end.

The downsides

I know speakers who refuse point blank to do question and answer sessions, but not because they are scared. It is much more about having a limited time to put your message across, so you choose to use it wisely. If you have a lot of content to fit into an hour, why rush it so that you leave 10 minutes at the end for a pedestrian, and often largely irrelevant, interaction?

Audiences often handle question and answer sessions badly as well. Either they are too shy to ask questions, resulting in that horrible silence as the speaker shifts from foot to foot, wondering if anyone will crack; or else the floor is opened to a loudmouth with a personal agenda.

So you see, the conventions of delivering a question and answer session need to be challenged. You really have to think hard about whether it will add anything.

A word to the wise though. If you decide you are going to break with this modern tradition, it is probably better to front this up in a positive way at some point. Towards the end of your presentation, something like this might be appropriate: 'I've covered a lot of ground today and it may be that some of you have questions. In your packs, you'll find a copy of the slides I've used, along with some supporting notes, which should answer most of your queries. I'll also be around throughout the coffee break if there's anything you'd like to ask...' Then carry on with your presentation through to the end.

Tip
Never, never, never!

Never take questions during a presentation. It will hijack your content, spoil the flow, ruin your timings and throw you off balance. A focused discussion group is the place for questions and answers, not your carefully prepared speech.

Tips for success

If you do think it is a good idea to have a question and answer session, here are some handy tips to help you make the most of it:

- Don't be afraid. Lots of speakers are terrified that when they throw it open to the floor someone will ask a question they don't know the answer to. This really should not be a problem.

First, you put the content together, so presumably have some insight into the subject you are talking about. If you don't know the exact answer to what they are asking, but feel it is legitimate to offer an educated guess, or your personal opinion, then do so, saying that's exactly what it is. If you have said what you think the answer is in your view, you can always throw this back to the questioner and ask 'Does that make sense? Is that what you think too?' If you really don't know the answer, then say so, but pledge to find out and make sure you do.

- Be prepared. If you have put the presentation together yourself, you will know the bits that are easy to explain and where the more complicated areas lie. Think about this when you are writing the content and you will probably be able to second guess the people in your audience; you will be able to spot the areas where they might want further clarification. They can be a right selfish lot, members of an audience. For example, if you are outlining plans to streamline a function of the company, they are less likely to ask about how that will affect the cost base, or the ongoing implications for customers and more likely to ask 'What will that mean for me?'

- Be even more prepared. When the moment arrives to let people in the audience have their say, we all know that terrible feeling of silence as tumbleweed blows through the auditorium. You can avoid this in several ways. Agree up front with a plant (a trusted colleague) that he or she will get the ball rolling with the first question. Alternatively, whoever is hosting the session might be prepared to step in. In both of these cases, there is a good chance that the audience will spot your bit of advance stage management, but that's better than the silence. Failing this you can have a selection of pre-prepared questions that you introduce. Use one of the following to lead you in: 'Often when I talk about this subject, people ask me afterwards, why do you...?' Or 'When Kim first asked me to speak on this subject, she was keen to know the answer to...' If they still don't take the bait after this, you can legitimately wrap the thing up and all go for coffee, where, incidentally, you will be collared by a succession of people who have questions they would like you to answer.

- When a question is asked, you can give yourself some thinking time by repeating it back. This will also ensure that the rest of the audience has heard it. A technical point to note is that in large venues it is best to have a couple of roaming radio microphones. Get people to raise their hand if they have a question and dispatch one of your audio people to get a microphone to them, so the audience isn't wondering what's going on.

Tip

Mostly, audiences are not looking to catch you out. Now and again, if the mood is hostile, there will be someone who nominates themselves as a 'spokesperson for the people', even though in reality they're often only representing their own militant views.

Activity

In a small, controlled environment, such as a team meeting, set up an opportunity to rehearse your technique for questions and answers. Presenting a new idea to your colleagues and then asking for any questions will help to build your confidence for a bigger platform.

Summary points

- Having a question and answer session has become the norm, but you have every right to challenge this and opt out if you wish.

- Always keep questions and answers for the end of your presentation, otherwise it will interrupt your flow and make it hard for the audience to follow.

- To avoid an embarrassing silence have some questions already prepared that you can answer as a lead in to proper audience interaction.

- If you don't know the answer, say so – this is much better than trying to bluff your way out of the situation.

15

Getting ready – some practical aspects

Most of the focus so far has been on responding to the brief, putting together a good presentation, making sure you are comfortable with it and coping with what you think you might have to deal with on the day. This isn't the only part of presenting though. There are also some practical but very important preparations to be made, well in advance if at all possible. Let's take a look at the things we need to do to get ready, starting with how you will look on the day.

Dress code

There is no set dress code for a presentation and I'm not about to try and impose one on you. What I will say, though, is that it matters. Maybe it shouldn't – after all, there is more to us than how we appear. But however much we might argue that this is a superficial way of judging people, it is a reality. Most of us would think twice about how we appear before a first date or a job interview and presentations are no different. Even before we've opened our mouths, we have sent a signal to the audience and they have started judging us.

Rather than tell you what to wear, I've outlined some thoughts below on the impact of the look you might choose. It's up to you to decide which route you want to go down.

Power dressing

This is all about status and confidence. I think of it as your 'Sunday best'. It's you at your smartest – your newest, best-fitting suit, for example. In a room full of other 'suits' it will make you fit in. In a setting where the norm is more casual, it will make you stand out. If you feel happy in what you're wearing this will make you feel more self-assured.

Personality dressing

If you're the outgoing, gregarious type, you may want the audience to get a sense of your individuality by how you appear. There is nothing wrong with a bit of creative expression, but take into account it may not be everyone's cup of tea and on that basis you might have to win them over with your sparkling insight and knowledge of the subject matter.

Costume dressing

Sometimes we might choose to dress for impact in a way which is congruent with what we are saying. I once saw mountaineer and adventurer Bear Grylls address an audience full of school teachers wearing his Everest-conquering red overalls, complete with ropes and other gear. The content of his speech was about his ascent to the summit and the subsequent lessons we could all learn about teamwork, resilience and so on.

Make a decision on whether you want to conform or 'rebel' and be confident in how you look. If you are comfortable, both in the sense of your attire being a good fit and in the impression you wish to make, then you're good to go.

It is not always the case that you have to mirror your audience. If you are conducting part of a training session, the audience may feel it's OK for them to turn up in jeans, as it's not a formal work day, but might still expect that you will be dressed for business.

Remember that a small number of well-tailored garments is better than a large collection of 'tat', so splash out on your 'stage wear' and make yourself feel good.

Real power dressing

Laurence was sales director of a company manufacturing window blinds and curtains.

While liaising with a major supplier over the launch of a new range of fabrics he was called to an important meeting with them and felt he should make the effort to dress appropriately.

On the day, he turned up wearing an immaculate suit, tailored from the new curtain material. That's how to power dress!

Equipment

Aside from what you are wearing, the checklist of what to take to a presentation will depend on the sort of gig it is. An internal company meeting, attended by a handful of your peers, won't need the same amount of equipment as a conference address to a room of 200 guests.

When you are really good at presentations, you will just be able to turn up on your own, confident in your ability and prepared to stand and talk off the cuff for however long is required. As your skills improve, you will find that a few well-constructed cue cards in your jacket pocket or handbag will provide all the insurance policy you need. Other than that, you will be happy to rely on your innate ability.

At the other end of the spectrum, where you have been booked to conduct a full-day seminar on your specialist subject, with all the attendant bells and whistles that are part of the modern presentation kit, you might decide to carry more gear than a rock band on a world tour.

Certainly, with unfamiliar venues and people you may not have dealt with until now, employing a belt and braces approach is a good idea. Whatever they have told you they can supply, take it as read that they'll forget; then you will be prepared for anything. I have never gone quite so far as taking my own flipchart easel, but many times I have taken spare pads with me and fresh new felt pens are a must, as it is a golden rule that any hotel's conference facility only contains pens with enough ink left to write up the title of a chart.

If PowerPoint is your thing, then obviously the least you need to do is carry a set of the slides with you in electronic format. If you trust the contact at the conference facility, you can arrange to e-mail the presentation in advance, so that they can load it up for you, ready to go when you arrive.

Good idea

If you're using PowerPoint or similar, don't rely on a single source for your slides. Instead have them saved to the cloud and also on a range of devices; smartphone, laptop, or tablet. This will prevent 'compatibility' issues with the technology.

Power might be an issue, so take items that are fully charged, have spare batteries where appropriate and take an electrical extension lead with multiple points to plug into. Strong parcel or gaffer tape is also a must, as you might have to set up some way from an electrical point and tape down any trailing wires.

Good idea

If you are being called on to do more and more presentations, at remote venues, with facilities you can never be sure of, then think about investing in your own, portable technical equipment. Take a look at the latest data projectors and consider a mobile sound system, using a 'tie clip' mic and powered speaker. With all of this 'gear', make sure you've tested it at home and familiarized yourself with how it works.

When it comes to handouts and resources (any props, prompts, paper exercises or physical kit that you need to distribute), take more copies than you need. The extra 'wasted' cost is worth it, as insurance against not having enough, and if you are clever you will find a way of reusing the materials at a later date. Expecting the venue's staff to be able to photocopy any extras is a dangerous game. Even if they can and they deliver them to your presentation suite before you get started, it is still bound to cost you dearly.

Assembling a kit of stationery items is useful. You never know when you are going to need the following:

- stapler (having checked it is fully loaded);
- pencils, sharpener and eraser;
- pens;
- hole punch and treasury tags;
- rule;
- reusable adhesive putty and masking tape (for attaching flipcharts to walls).

Coming up is advice on how to compile a delivery schedule for each presentation. When you have done this, you should add all your regular items of equipment, as a tick-box checklist. Use the template each time your prepare a presentation. It is better to take more than you think you will need.

When you don't have any gigs lined up for a while, store all your presentation kit together, so that you don't have to search round the house for the component parts. Plastic storage boxes that collapse down flat are available at good DIY stores and are ideal for carting this sort of stuff around in. It also means that after you have set up at the venue you can fold the boxes away.

As an aside, when you are self-contained like this, it means shifting and carrying quite a lot of kit. Make sure you check in advance with hotels and conference facilities that you can park close to where you will be setting up. This is particularly important in city centre venues, where parking restrictions might apply.

Once you have set up all the technical kit, make sure you tidy anything else away, out of sight, so your audience cannot see what you have brought. Use a long table, positioned behind where you will stand to lay out any giveaways or handouts and put them in the order you will come across them in the presentation. There's nothing worse than juggling bits of paper, or not being able to find the handout you are looking for.

The hardware you might need will vary from one presentation to another, but the constant in all of this is the confidence you feel from being well prepared. The more variables there are, the more important it is to control the things you can. With forethought, planning and a comprehensive kit of parts, you will always look and feel like a professional. It is a good idea to make a checklist for the day. Table 15.1 gives a useful example.

Table 15.1   Checklist for PowerPoint presentations

Equipment/things to do	Check
Have I e-mailed the presentation to my contact?	☐
Have I charged my laptop?	☐
Have I got:	
• a set of slides in electronic format?	☐
• my slides saved in the Cloud?	☐
• mains and connecting leads?	☐
• an electrical extension lead?	☐
• strong parcel or gaffer tape?	☐
• printed handouts of the presentation?	☐
• the name and contact number of the venue's technical person, for set-up?	☐
Have I checked the route to the venue and where I can park?	☐

Activity

Make your own presentation checklist, taking the suggestions from this chapter as a starting point and adding any extra items that are specific to your own sphere. Buy any outstanding items and keep them all together as part of your kit. The more comprehensive your own equipment is, the more you'll be in control. Remember to allow time to access the room you'll be speaking in; if you have technical items you will also need time to set them up.

Summary points

- Don't neglect the details of preparation, including how you will look on the day and what you will take with you.

- Dress appropriately and comfortably, then you can focus on the job in hand instead of worrying about what you are wearing.

- Assemble your own presentation kit. Keep all the items together, with a checklist, to tick off what is needed for each speech.

- Always take more handouts and resources than you need. It increases your confidence if you are prepared for anything and it makes you look more professional.

- If you are doing lots of presentations, it is worth investing in the technical kit you need – that way you can be guaranteed it will be working.

16

As the moment approaches

When the day of the presentation finally arrives, I hope it will dawn with you feeling a mixture of excitement, anticipation and a few nervous moments (which are good for keeping you sharp).

Here we look at the lead-up to your address, as well as examining some strategies for what to do when things don't quite go to plan. Armed with this knowledge, nothing can stop you.

The final countdown

I have purposely not put any measure on the countdown to your presentation, simply because the timescales for different presentations can be so variable. Instead, I have just given a sequence of events, adding here and there the ideal amount of time for a particular stage:

- **Preparation**
  This can involve anything from the receipt of a full written brief to an off-the-cuff request to speak. Whatever its form, this is the stage where you need to consider what the task is, who the audience will be and how you will deliver against the set objective.

- **Writing**
  If you are very good at speeches and have been asked to talk on your specialist subject, a few sketched notes will act as a

sufficient aide-memoire to the words you have probably spoken a thousand times before. At the other end of the spectrum, when you have been asked to deliver new content you may not be so familiar with, the writing stage is critical. Bear this in mind, as it will have an impact on how much time you need.

- **Rehearsal**

  If you want to get better, then get to know your material with full confidence, so you have more chance of concentrating on the 'performance'. Ideally, you should be fully rehearsed the day before you are due to present. My own preference is to have a final run through at home, or in the car on the way to the event just to double-check I know what I am going to say. After that I leave it alone. I have seen speakers sitting in a row on a platform, waiting for their turn and nervously shuffling through pages of notes. It's not a good look and betrays their lack of confidence.

- **Familiarization**

  This is the process I think of as the great 'nerve calmer'. Get to the venue with plenty of time to spare. Before a major presentation, it is unlikely you will be able to focus on any other pressing task, so devote yourself wholly to this issue – checking social media, incoming messages or your news feed can wait. Use the time before the presentation to get familiar with the layout of the room. Talk to the venue's technical people, find out what they expect and what they can offer. Check with your host on the detail of timings, how you will be announced and by whom. If you have had a chance to do all this in advance, then there is still no excuse for not arriving early. It can offer all sorts of benefits. You might pick up on some detail that you can work into your opening, about the venue itself or the local area. You might be able to meet some delegates in advance and sharing what they tell you with the wider audience can be a great way of engaging with the whole group. Or you may spend the time getting to know the other speakers or your host, all of which could lead to you being 'booked' again in the future.

- **Go with the flow**
  Now is not the time to be having a tantrum about the fact the lectern microphone is set at the wrong height, or that there were no puppies in your dressing room, as you had specified! It is too late; you just have to go with what is in front of you. In fact, in many ways the ability to be unfazed by anything the day might throw at you is the mark of a true professional.

- **Be charming and relaxed**
  Ha! Yeah, that's easy to say, isn't it? Quite naturally, as the moment approaches, you will become increasingly nervous, but often your hosts want to know they have booked the right man or woman, so pacing up and down and proclaiming loudly 'They always make me really nervous, these things!' is not likely to fill them (or you) with oodles of confidence. When you are up there on stage it is a bit like putting on an act, so add to your case for an Oscar by starting the process the minute you arrive at the venue.

- **Showtime**
  Immediately prior to being announced is the time when your heart will probably be beating fastest. If you have followed the golden rules of preparation and really nailed that opening, you will be fine, just remember that. Keep smiling, look confident – of course you can! – approach the podium, take your time and deliver that killer first line. After that it's easy, I promise you.

I wasn't expecting that!

Anyone who has done the rounds on the speaker circuit will tell you the same thing: if it can go wrong, it will. This is rather cold comfort for the rookie presenter who is not only terrified of getting up there, but also of mishaps.

Worst of all is when something happens that you were not expecting; then you really do have to think on your feet. Let's attempt to eradicate some of those situations by having a look at the common issues that arise.

Equipment meltdown

The most common thing to go wrong with presentations is the hardware. Do some basic checks when you get to the venue and make sure things are working the way you want them to.

Flick through your slides in a dummy run and check them against your notes. If there is a lectern with a mic attached, or you're wearing a 'tie clip' microphone, try to get in early enough to be able to sound check. Good technical people are a godsend in these circumstances, but not all presentations will have one, so you need to work out how this stuff works for yourself.

If you are faced with equipment meltdown, stay on the front foot as much as is humanly possible – just shrug, say it would have been nice to have the accompanying visuals, but it's no big deal. Don't keep referring wistfully to how much more wonderful this experience would have been if only the audience had been able to see slide 8, or 12, or 176; it's gone, let it go.

Even if you are taking a low-tech approach and are using a flip chart, you should still take the time to check that the easel is not wobbling and that you have sufficient pens.

The sky is falling

Call it an act of God or some such thing, but occasionally, during your presentation, you are faced with something entirely unexpected. I once had a ceiling tile cave in at the back of the room. It didn't hit anyone, but the noise it made caused a bit of a commotion. A fire alarm going off is more common than you would think. I have often wished I could make this happen with a remote control, during a presentation that's going badly! Delegates fainting, waiters wandering in and walking across your eye-line, shouts, laughter, or the sound of aircraft flying overhead; you name it, it can happen. Most common is a mobile going off. When that happens, I carry on regardless and pretend I can't hear it; it's the idiot who forgot to switch it off who then suffers! Take it as it comes. If it is minor, ignore it. If not, deal with it as quickly as possible and move on.

Mis-communication

I am a bit loathe to put this in as a heading, but I suppose I have to as it is so commonplace. Or is it? Usually the 'breakdown in communication' is a universal excuse to cover up for the fact that someone screwed up. It is still a good idea to try and eradicate it, by making sure that the communications that are issued from *your* end are clear, concise and unequivocal.

You don't have to be officious when you discuss your requirements as a speaker, but it's fine to be firm. Try to confirm everything in writing and ask that the organizers acknowledge what you have sent them. I always find it a great help if the organisation you are presenting to nominates a project manager, someone who will oversee all your requirements. You cannot force them to do this, but you can at least ask for a point of contact who will guide you on the day of the presentation itself.

Summarizing all the key information about a presentation is a good way of ensuring that communication happens effectively. Sometimes you will be sent this information in the form of a delivery schedule by whoever has booked you, but if not you need to be proactive: compile your own and send it to key people at the venue. An example is shown in Figure 16.1.

Here's a quick reminder of some dos and don'ts, which can serve as a quick reminder and hopefully also a confidence booster, before you stand up to speak.

Figure 16.1   Sample delivery schedule

Delivery schedule

Client:	Health Systems plc
Venue:	Western House Brighton Street Wolford W1 VCX
Date and time:	14.12.2022 – 09:30
Contact:	Richard Lazarus 0661 4661 (office) 07476 112 (mobile)
Type of event:	National sales conference
Speaker requirements:	Laptop Data projector PowerPoint Flipchart and pens
Room layout:	'Cabaret' style (10 delegates per table)

Five deadly sins

Don't apologise for who you are, what you say, how you sound, what you look like or anything else. All you'll do is draw the attention of the audience away from the message you're delivering.

Avoid complacency at all costs. Taking a presentation, or even worse, an audience for granted, just because you've delivered the content a hundred times or know the people in the room, doesn't mean you can switch off from the business of engaging them; if you do, then they certainly will.

Stop trying to be who you're not. Whoever the greatest orators of all time were, you are not their tribute act, you are you, only ever that person. Over time, you'll come to realise that even if you've got 'weaknesses' in presenting, people will overlook them to get to the authentic version of you.

Bluff and bluster will find you out during a Q&A, so just be honest. If you don't know the answer say so, but also be comfortable in supplementing this with an 'in my opinion' type answer.

Never forget that the audience is the most important thing and it's their needs you're there to satisfy. Focussing on anything else is a waste of time and will take you down a road to failure.

Five golden rules

Be real and be realistic. Stay true to yourself and don't expect miracles from any presentation; instead set a goal of getting through it, communicating in plain language and learning from the experience.

Other people's failings don't excuse your bad behaviour. If what you were expecting from others, on the day of the presentation, doesn't materialize, then park your upset, get on and deliver to the best of your ability, and hold an inquest later, in a calm and professional manner.

Practice makes perfect is an adage that's as old as the hills, but it's no less relevant for that. Even when things don't go entirely to plan with a presentation, not all is lost. Remember, it was just another opportunity to hone your skills.

Stay true to what you've planned and don't let others derail that by moving the goalposts. By all means build some flexibility into your speech, in terms of length or content, but deliver what was asked in the brief, not on the basis of a last-minute whim.

Minimize the risk of failure by controlling as much of the external environment and logistical issues as you can, especially the big things. Plan to do this well in advance, and if there's a minor blip on the day, you'll be better equipped to deal with it.

Activity

Draw up a delivery schedule. You can base it on the example shown if you wish. When you use it in practice, be sure to number and date each version, so if the situation changes, at either end, you can be certain both parties are working off the same sheet.

Summary points

- Go through the stages of preparation fully and you will feel confident about what you are going to present.

- Arrive early. It gives you a chance to familiarize yourself with the venue and to settle in.

- Be prepared for things going wrong; they sometimes do and it is the sign of a professional presenter if you can rise above this.

- Ensure that all your communication prior to the event is clear and unambiguous, to avoid too many surprises on the day.

17
Stripped bare

There is a level of presentation skill we all aspire to, being able to stand before an audience without any tools, notes or cues and deliver a seamless address without missing a beat.

This chapter looks at the art of presenting, stripped bare. We'll examine the risks and the benefits as well as considering how it can be achieved. Let's begin though by looking at a rationale for taking the risk: what are the 'fors' and 'againsts'?

Why not?

For most of us the thought of having nothing to fall back on when we are presenting is intimidating to say the least, but why is that? We already know that if we trace the fear of presentations back to its roots, the one thing we are most scared of is looking foolish. In front of our peers or customers we are afraid of drying up, saying the wrong thing entirely, losing our thread and generally coming across as incompetent. There is the added fear that without structure our presentation won't keep to time or stay on message.

Why?

Taking a more positive stance, the main reasons for choosing to deliver in this way are the counterpoints to the risks. An audience can recognize how difficult a task it is to deliver without accompaniment and this in itself is an impressive feat. It signals that you are brave, passionate and accomplished; it says you are sufficiently sure of your ground to not need any 'outside' help. Paradoxically perhaps, they are more likely to be forgiving of 'mistakes', and this is a factor which immediately starts to ameliorate some of the risk. If things do seem to go a little off script they will make allowances for this, balancing it against the fact that what they are getting is genuinely 100 per cent you.

Overcoming the fear of exposure

Sitting having coffee with friends most of us wouldn't hesitate to tell a story which illustrated the topic under discussion and a presentation stripped bare is simply a scaled up version of this. What underlies our fear is in fact illogical: we are afraid we won't be able to deliver and yet we do it all the time; the only difference is the size and make up of the audience.

Perceptions of audiences

As we have already discovered in Chapter 2, once an audience reaches a certain size the addition of extra people makes no real difference. In the coffee scenario we feel comfortable 'holding court' with perhaps up to a dozen people. It can be just as embarrassing making a gaffe in front of that many as an audience of 100 so the numbers are not really important.

There is a point at which an audience, in the eyes of a nervous presenter, becomes an amorphous mass. The reality is audiences are made up of *individuals* and if we think of presenting to one person, the whole task gets easier.

Expectation

Similarly, as we have seen, audiences can be as varied as the people in them and judging the situation in advance is one of the toughest jobs we face. There is a world of difference between proposing a toast at a family occasion and addressing the staff at the annual conference. Their issues are not the same, nor is their 'advance engagement'.

Flying solo, without the aid of the usual presentation support mechanisms, can be even more powerful in a situation which is a little adversarial. We recognize that there are risks, but winning an audience over might be better done by presenting yourself as open and vulnerable than by hiding behind a lectern and a couple of dozen slides.

Achievement

If you are still not convinced of the benefits of presenting this way, consider what you might achieve by doing it.

Whatever it is you say, this is only a small part of a presentation. Often style has a way of complementing substance (it is rarely, if ever, a substitute!) Standing alone on a stage signals your self-confidence to an audience; it says, 'Look, this is me and this is what I have to say.' Confidence is a trait which is much better judged from the outside than the inside. We may not be feeling at our most bullish, but if we can pull off a tolerable performance without too many glitches, other people will perceive us as competent. Ultimately, we will attain the status of a consummate professional.

Preparing to succeed

Nothing to lose

What's the worst that can happen? You probably have a long list of disaster scenarios in your head but they are unlikely to come to pass if a bit of thought and preparation goes into the project. Sometimes nervous presenters have an image of perfection in their heads and if they don't live up to this they consider it a failure.

An audience is just people, they know things go wrong, they are aware of the difficulties of presentations and they rarely expect perfection.

Sometimes a bit of vulnerability goes a long way with an audience; it shows you are human. Treat glitches with good humour, don't be tempted to criticize and have an attitude which says, 'let's carry on regardless.' Resilience can be an appealing trait too.

Develop spontaneity

Although presenting without any supporting aids can be intimidating at first, it is a great way of putting yourself on the spot. Although this is the reason so few people are prepared to attempt it, what you do find quite quickly is how to deal with the unexpected; you're forced into it.

Just as a great comedian becomes a master of the ad lib, so you too get to a stage where you are able to handle pretty much anything which comes your way. Not only is this a great skill to acquire but it also has the benefit of high-level audience engagement. Don't we all love to see someone triumph over adversity?

Advanced memory tips

One of the greatest fears with this kind of venture is that we will stand in front of an expectant audience and forget everything we intended to say. Here, as reinforcement of what we have already outlined in Chapters 4 and 8, are some *extra* memory techniques.

Work the material

If you have left yourself sufficient preparation time for your speech you should have it developed and written well in advance. This gives you the luxury of running some of it past an audience. I've mentioned finding a trusted colleague or friend who would be prepared to listen and give you feedback and in itself this is no bad idea. However, it lacks the authenticity of a *real* audience. You have already prompted your 'listener' and they are probably desperate to give you *positive* feedback.

Another advanced technique is to take parts of the speech and 'slip them into conversation'. This can be particularly useful if you are attempting humour. Clearly you can only do this with snatches of the speech but it gives you a chance for a try-out in a safe environment. If people laugh you can be confident in keeping those lines in; if it's more serious subject matter, try to gauge a reaction in terms of engagement.

Performance is rehearsal

Some speeches we make are a one-off but there are also instances where we can use the content time and time again. We re-visit practical examples of this shortly in 'Creating standard material'. Let us say you are asked to present on your specialist subject, for the sake of argument 'using social media to win more business'. The first time you deliver it you may be too nervous to take much account of audience reaction, but over time as the presentation flows more smoothly you should get a sense of the things that generally go down well and the parts which are less engaging. Count this process as a rehearsal for the next time you have to deliver and you will improve with each occasion.

Use a mnemonic

The three-part rule of constructing a speech applies more than ever when you are going to be unscripted. Giving each of these sections its own key word is a way of leading you in. Save for the odd politician, most of us can remember three words! Using alliteration might help but so can making up a word.

A vital cue

The topic of the presentation is how to use social media to promote your business. Your overall message is about the frequency and quality of messages and the need to keep them in line with customers' existing expectations. The three points you'll make are around Content (and how to maintain the quality of what you put out), how Often you post (tying back to your point about frequency), and the need to be Brand consistent, so customers relate to what you're saying. Your three letters form the word COB (content, often, brand) and that outline is fixed in your head.

The kitchen is not your stage

Wherever you choose to rehearse – driving in the car, while running on the treadmill, or when making a cup of tea – none of it will ever match the feeling we get when we're standing up in front of the real live audience. This is one of the reasons for emphasizing repetition in the rehearsal process. No matter how well you think you know it an extra run through will be of benefit. The only rule is to have a cut off point around an hour before you are due to speak so you have time to gather yourself together. As I have already said, rehearsing right up to the point when you are announced can increase anxiety and be more of a hindrance than a help.

You will forget!

In coaching hundreds of speakers over many years, the question they most often ask is 'but what happens if I do forget something?' The answer is always the same, 'you will!' The real issue from a professional presentational point of view is whether or not the audience will know. Once we accept there is a likelihood we will forget, it removes some of the pressure and as long as we can keep going no one but us will ever know.

They don't know what you're going to say!

Creating standard material

We are familiar with the feelings of nervousness which occur when first standing up to speak, but in the main these subside quickly once we're into the flow. This is why I have suggested constructing a standard opening which can be adapted to different circumstances. Apart from saving the time and trouble of thinking of a new beginning for each speech, it will get you over the early nerves. By the same token I have recommended building up a collection of stories to fall back on. Over time you can develop a bank of content relevant to your industry or job role. Universal stories like the necessity to keep up our social media presence, the pace of change in business, or managing information overload will always come in handy and can sometimes be 'fed in' at an appropriate moment. Having a store of stories also gives you some leeway when it comes to timing: if you think you're going to fall short of your allotted slot, you can 'fill' with an appropriate anecdote – just make sure it's relevant.

How to open

In Chapter 10 I outlined the importance of a strong opening and this is never more so than when you are going to go unscripted. There are dozens of ways you can begin a speech and whichever you choose the advice is the same as before: make sure you know it off by heart. Be true to your personality, don't flatter or flannel if you haven't got anything genuinely good to say but if you truly have had a positive experience at this event or venue in the past it's a good strong way of opening. Here are three examples.

1 When X asked me if I'd come and speak to you today I jumped at the chance, otherwise I'd be sitting at home watching daytime television!

2 One of the difficulties we all face in business today is having too much time on our hands and not enough to do.

3 I always love coming to (name of town) because it reminds me of (anecdote about previous visit).

We have talked before about the benefits of a story which is self-deprecating. This is one of my personal favourites – it helps that it is true.

'The last time I did this was at a wedding and afterwards a woman approached me and said, "When they announced it was time for the speeches my heart sank!" I quickly interjected and said I was sorry if it had spoiled her day. "Oh no", she replied, "you weren't nearly as boring as I thought you were going to be!"

It is perhaps my best testimonial so far.'

With plenty of experience we develop a kind of filing system in our heads where we store the content which we have collected over a period of time. This can then be mixed and matched to create new presentations, opening with a line about the current economic conditions, telling a story about the effects of organizational culture, following this with three main points about the changes we all face in the workplace and wrapping up with an amusing anecdote about a social media post that caused a stir.

Just because you have read a chapter about advanced level presentation skills this doesn't mean it will take away all the fears of presenting 'unplugged': it is only practice which will do this. Start small, don't be too ambitious at first, know where you are going, have a back-up plan (some cue cards in your pocket as an insurance policy) and be both human and yourself. After that it's easy.

Summary points

- Preparation is the key to success.
- Professionalism builds in direct proportion to time spent 'on stage'.
- Do your best to remember; don't fret if you forget.
- Presenting without aids is hard, but the rewards are worth it.

18
Advanced interactivity

There is a degree of interactivity in *all* presentations and we examined the basics of this in Chapter 13. You speak, they listen, it's sort of interactive. However, recent technological developments have led us to realize that rich, real time interactivity can now be a part of any address. It has caused us to think again about relating to audiences and getting feedback. There is now an opportunity for *advanced* interactivity.

In this chapter we will look at more ways we can involve our audience with techniques as old as the Q & A, through to instant reaction via a Twitter feed. We will consider the pluses and minuses and examine ways of controlling the process so you don't cede the power of your presentation to the audience.

The trouble with feedback

For most people in business the word 'feedback' is steeped in negativity. If we hear the phrase 'can you come into my office, I want to give you some feedback' the immediate reaction of a majority of people is 'what have I done wrong?' And yet we know that logic dictates we can only improve our own performance if we are able to get a real sense of what an audience thinks. Aside from the potential for praise or criticism it is an opportunity to check understanding; is their interpretation of our message the same as our original intention? Have we missed anything? Was the style and complexity right?

Feedback forms (sometimes called 'happy sheets') are the bane of most presenters' lives too. If the assembled throng have been asked to comment on our performance, the first reaction for most of us is to riffle through looking for the negatives. Often a single unhappy 'customer' can undo all the good of a hundred who were delighted.

Try to see feedback as your friend, a way of checking not only that today went OK, but for shaping tomorrow too.

Is it dangerous?

Many people are fearful of asking an audience's opinion because they don't want to hear the bad news. This is short-sighted as presentations shouldn't be seen as a survival course where you do your bit and hope to get off the stage unscathed; instead they are a real and vital opportunity to make a connection.

If interactivity can be judged to be 'dangerous' it is only because we cannot predict with certainty the reaction we will get. However, with forethought and planning much can be done to head off a potential disaster.

Is it helpful?

If you think your message is significant enough to want people to remember it then 'engagement' is an imperative. The sure-fire way of doing this is to think of the presentation as a two-way street, not something where you simply dump your views on them. This can only be done through some form of interaction. Let's examine some ways of executing this.

A range of interactive techniques

The first thing to say about getting a response is it is much easier if there is safety in numbers. If you ask the audience 'does anyone have an example of poor communication they can share with us?' it entails a single individual having the courage to suddenly turn themselves into 'presenter'. Contrast this with the simple 'show of hands' I talked about in Chapter 13. Whatever the reaction, you can usually create a fitting quip.

Figure 18.1   Interactivity tools

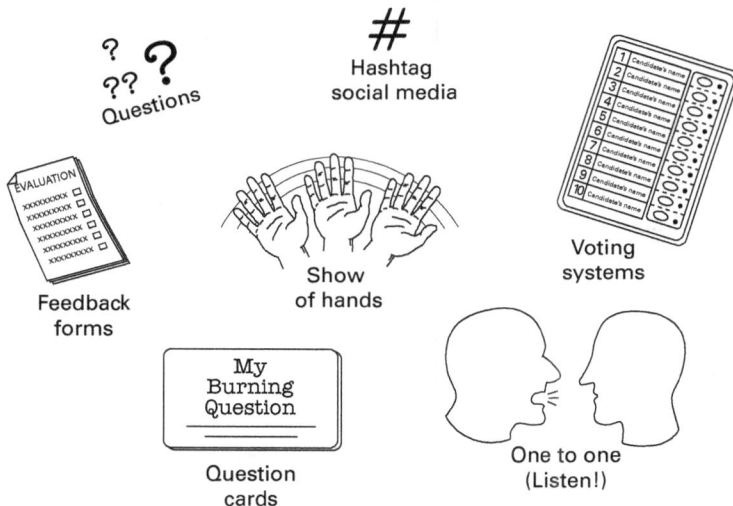

1. Ask questions

I've talked about one of the simplest ways of drawing an audience towards you: ask them a question, then yours is not the only voice that's heard. I'd caution once again that you are careful with this technique. First, make sure it's planned. An off-the-cuff question might seem like a good idea but could lead you down a blind alley.

Unless you have good reason to, don't ask a question too early in the presentation (see the upcoming section 'Warming them up to interactivity'). Always keep the possible answers as simple as you can: tying an audience member up in knots will work against you in the engagement stakes.

Think ahead

An important part of questioning is being prepared for *any* response. Let us say you are speaking on 'How to get the best out of e-mail' and you ask the following question:

'How do we think we might use e-mail better?'

What do you do if you get any of the following?

a No response at all.

b A range of helpful suggestions.

c A maverick answer; for example, 'We should ban all e-mail from now on.'

Unless you prepare yourself for a wide range of responses (including complete silence) you risk being thrown off track, so make sure you have a follow-up strategy for each set of circumstances.

If you feel a more structured level of interaction is required then refer back to the advice on setting up a formal Q & A session at the end of your speech.

2. Use a voting system

Some venues have the facility to use a voting system, with keypads made available to every audience member. However, more usual now is the hashtag/app/URL form of interaction, where each delegate can communicate with the on-stage speaker in real time. This allows all sorts of possibilities for interaction and is now very commonplace. It's a useful way of conducting a Q & A, especially if there is a facilitator on hand who can quickly vet, summarize and group the questions together, ensuring the most common ones get asked and answered.

3. Advance set-up

Sometimes you can get your audience to do some work beforehand. If you are holding an internal company conference the delegate list will be compiled well in advance and so will the programme of topics. You can e-mail something to the delegates before your speech to prompt their thoughts. This helps to manage their expectation and act as a catalyst on the day, so you won't be starting from 'cold'. Here is an example:

The big 3!

'At next week's conference I will be talking about our sales effort next year. My presentation will be called "The big 3" because I believe there are 3 key things we will need to do to meet our targets. Help me out, by thinking of your 'Big 3'. Bring them along on the day and we'll have an opportunity to share our ideas.'

You may not have sufficient time or insider knowledge for this, but a simplified version might be to have 'burning question' cards in the registration area. As guests arrive your team can be prompted to ask them to fill these out and leave them in a box. This gives you the chance to see their issues ahead of your speech and it takes the pressure off individuals who may not want to raise their hand and ask out loud.

4. Post-match analysis

When it comes to feedback forms, rather than a 'tick box' exercise try to think creatively. By now you know the importance of understanding an audience and one thing which is common to most people is a desire to get away when an event has finished; many will have a long commute or may want to return to their desks. The last thing most people want to do is fill out a detailed questionnaire about your presentation.

How then do we get away from just having a few random ticks on a sheet of paper? One way of doing this is to ask delegates for 'one word feedback', an open exercise where they can write anything they like to describe the session (from experience, many take the time to write longer comments). During a longer event, don't save the feedback right for the end. Prior to afternoon coffee you can prompt delegates to fill in their feedback during the break. You can use the line, 'if you'd like to get ahead of the game, please feel free to fill in your feedback forms over coffee.' It is much more likely you will get richer, more detailed comments if people don't feel under pressure to 'hit the road'.

If at all possible, you should try to follow up on feedback so people don't feel it was a waste of time. Ask for suggestions as well as assessment or critique and e-mail or contact those who have taken the time to pass comment.

5. Use a

Many large conferences now use a specific hashtag (#) on Twitter/X related to the event. This can be a great way of capturing audience opinion over the course of a day, or even during a specific speech.

You may need some advance set-up to advise delegates this tool will be used and an explanation at the start of the day for those who are not familiar with the technology, but it is well worth it in terms of quality interaction, especially so as it happens in real time.

> The larger the audience, the less likely people are to raise a hand to forward their point of view; however, using social media you can get instant responses to what you are saying.
>
> *'I have outlined our customer charter, based on what we currently think, but maybe there's something missing? Pair up with the person next to you, have a chat for the next five minutes and see if you can come up with anything new, then post it at #kpconference and we'll take a look at a selection of the suggestions.'*

6. Hang around and chat

This seems obvious but many presenters dash for the door the minute they finish, just in case they get 'collared' by someone who took issue with what was said. Where possible, use the less formal time after a presentation to gather the views of audience members. This is harder if you are last on stage at a conference, but if you are guest speaker at an evening event for a professional body, ask that you go on first and have the buffet supper afterwards. This gives people a chance to approach you and discuss their feelings. If people liked what you did, their positive feedback can provide a great confidence boost.

7. Play the long game

We live in such an instantaneous world we have come to expect everything to happen right now! It is true that after most events or speeches there is a law of diminishing returns once they have finished. People tend to give a 'knee-jerk' reaction and then move on to the next thing. However, you may be in a situation where you conduct a quarterly address to colleagues. Under these circumstances it is useful to keep an open dialogue going during the time *between* events. In this way you can show your audience you have listened to their suggestions or concerns, followed up afterwards and amended your actions to take account of what they said.

One reason many people dislike feedback is they see it as a 'vanity' exercise on the part of the speaker. If instead you turn it into a 'conversation' over a longer period, they will be much more likely to stay engaged with the process and offer their thoughts more readily.

Warming them up to interactivity

We know audiences can often be reserved, particularly early in the day when they haven't been warmed up, and this will limit their propensity to join in, which makes interactivity a bit difficult. The way you treat them can have a big effect here: if they feel they are being cajoled or even intimidated into a response they may back off even more.

Use simple techniques to get them on your side. First, don't scare them by being too 'in their face'. Lead in gently and get them on your side before you attempt the riskier aspects of presenting. Remove barriers as much as possible, don't hide behind a lectern or a wad of notes, try to use open gestures with your hands to 'welcome them in' and smile as much as is reasonable! Put some energy into your performance, look and act passionate and make it appear that you are enjoying yourself – they are much more likely to engage then. When it comes to language, keep it informal and remember to use lots of inclusive phrases, things like 'we all hate poor customer service, don't we?', or 'which of us hasn't felt like getting on our soapbox from time to time?'

Great speakers involve the people they address and as with many techniques we get better at doing this over time. Expect the unexpected and build your experience of interaction.

Summary points

- Interactivity is the best way of engaging an audience.
- Welcome feedback: it helps you develop better presentations.
- Treat your audience with respect; don't intimidate them.
- Choose a method you know will work, whether simple voting or complex interaction.

19
Progress report

I have deliberately steered away from setting targets in this book. Yes, goal setting is important, but how you do that is up to you. Base it on where you are now, how far you want to travel and how fast.

All this chapter does is suggest some ways you can monitor your progress. Seeking other people's opinion will be a large part of this, but we are in an area of subjectivity, so take as wide a range of measures as possible to try and get a realistic perspective on how you are doing.

You are the best judge

For most things in life, we can usually tell when we have done well or badly. If you play sport, you know the instant you leave the field of play whether you have had a good game or not. The same is true if you make a presentation. Get into the habit of thinking of your presentation as three separate speeches. Before you go on stage, visualize what it will be like; second, do the speech itself; and third, look back on how it actually was. If you think about the differences between your expectations, your experience and your hindsight you can begin to understand where the gaps are from what you planned, to what you delivered, to what the audience received.

Record and review

Film your performance on your phone whenever you can. All your energy and attention when you are presenting is focused on performing to the best of your ability; there's little room left to objectively assess how you're doing. By watching yourself back afterwards, you get a true sense of how the audience saw you; it's full of valuable lessons.

Quickly put aside your discomfort over how you look and sound and instead try to focus objectively on your performance as a whole. When did you rush things too much? At what point did the audience laugh and why? How could you edit the content down to make it even tighter? These are the sort of questions you should be asking yourself.

When you have answered them, by all means go back to the subject of how you appear and the way your voice comes across, but see it from the audience's point of view. Are you engaging, interesting and entertaining? If you have still got some work to do, try to make the changes over time, then film yourself again, so you can start the loop of continuous improvement.

Ask the people who matter

Be careful who you listen to. Presenting badly is a blow to the confidence and a dent in your ego. For this reason, the people who like you might want to protect you from the truth. They will tell you it was fine, when really it wasn't.

The other side of the coin is the resentful colleague who recognizes you did a good job, but will never admit it. Toxic feedback plays on your self-confidence and makes it harder to get up and do it all again.

Audience reaction

A positive audience reaction tells its own story, but even if this doesn't happen, it might not be that they don't like you. I have delivered the same speech, twice in one week, to different audiences and had completely different reactions. What was really frustrating about this was after the second address, during the coffee break, half a dozen different people approached me and said how much they had enjoyed what I had done. Tempted as I was to say, 'Well next time, why don't you let your face show it?', I simply thanked them instead and concluded just because they don't look like they love you, doesn't mean that they hate you. A good lesson, that one.

Future bookings

Often you will find that speaking as an invited guest at an event leads to being approached to speak at others in the future. If this happens you can be sure you must have put on a good performance. At some point, people will be happy to pay you for your services and when that day comes, you realize you have arrived as a speaker.

With this in mind, always have some business cards to hand or some way people can contact you. Try not to get drawn into negotiation there and then. It is much better to do this away from the noise of the crowd, so suggest instead that you meet or telephone in the next day or so.

Formal feedback

I've highlighted the fact that at many events and conferences, there will be a written evaluation form for delegates to complete. Try using the advanced techniques discussed to improve the quality of this, but at the very least you can be sure of getting a set of scores to reflect upon. There is often a space for comments too, and this can be where you find the most valuable feedback of all.

Whatever the outturn of the feedback, treat it objectively. We've recognized that at the end of a long day, most delegates want to race for the car and hit the road homewards. They're often not very concerned with 'giving their feedback', so you should judge the scores with this in mind.

This is why I have said we are always drawn to the most negative end of the spectrum. If 199 delegates give you 10 out of 10, you will focus on the one remaining who scored you at 4.

Balance your approach here. Don't ignore negative comments altogether or this will result in the sort of arrogance which will stop you improving, but keep a sense of proportion: it's unlikely we will engage with all the people all of the time.

Take all the methods I've suggested for measuring your performance and begin to track them over time, then you start to build up a much more accurate picture of just how good a presenter you are.

To help you formalize and track your progress, the presentation analysis grid in Table 19.1 sets out some headings and asks you to fill in your marks, add comments and consider what you will do next. Some of the fields are filled in to give you an idea of what is required.

Table 19.1   Presentation analysis grid

Skill	Rating	Reflections	Actions
Content	7	*Too much content*	*Edit – ask 'what's the point?'*
Confidence	6	*Nervous at first, settled down quickly*	*More practice*
Presence			
Conviction	9	*Well-constructed arguments*	*More of this!*
Resilience			
Voice			
Body language	6	*Felt stilted*	*Try to relax*
Overall performance			

Activity

Map out some milestones over the short, medium and long term. Make the goals personal to you and keep them realistic, then decide when you wish to reach each stage by and chart your progress. You might consider goals such as 'Write 10 minutes on communication skills', 'Develop a writing template with key headings' or 'Deliver a short presentation without notes'.

It's a good idea to set your own agenda and consider carefully where your next challenge will be, to turn you into a successful presenter. In a work context, this will help you no matter what your job role and in other aspects of life, you'll become known as a trusted and capable speaker, able to deliver a few well chosen words, no matter what the occasion.

Summary points

- There's nothing like video and review for seeing yourself as others see you; it's a really powerful tool.

- Make time for personal reflection following each presentation and be honest about how your performance went.

- Take into account the views of as wide a group of people as possible when assessing your performance.

- Audience reaction is a great test for success. Did the audience enjoy it? Balance this with what people actually say afterwards.

- Take the positives out of the feedback forms and try to be objective about any negative comment.

- When you have assimilated all your measures of success, think about how you could be better next time.

20
Confidence under pressure

I spend a lot of time teaching presentation skills face to face, so this chapter is a consequence of that experience, drawing on how people feel in the real world when they're asked to present.

My starting point is to ask delegates about hopes and fears. The answers are nearly always the same: the hope is to 'not make a fool of myself'; the fear is 'making a fool of myself'. The topic which comes up more than any other is confidence, so taking some of the learning from earlier chapters and adding that to the experience of real managers in the workplace, this chapter will consider what confidence is, what it looks like and how we can get more of it.

It is also sometimes the case that we're asked to present at short notice; for example, at an interview, where we may not have been given the topic beforehand and we have a short time to prepare. So we will examine the area of presenting under pressure, by revisiting what we already know about structure and adding to it with the inclusion of a section on persuasion.

Building confidence

Let's begin with a dictionary definition of confidence: 'Confidence is the feeling or belief that one can have faith in or rely on someone or something.' We all know how a confident presenter looks when they're speaking: in command of their subject matter and comfortable in their own skin. But look again at the definition, especially the part that says 'feeling or belief'. In the early part of our presentation skills development we only have to *engender* that feeling or belief, no matter if we're less sure of ourselves than we might appear.

I can illustrate this through the real experiences of hundreds of managers. When we role-play presentations in the training room environment, they are always captured on video, so the presenter can watch their 'performance'. The reason this is important is that it's impossible to assess the way you're coming across while you're actually doing it. When you're standing up and delivering, you're much too distracted by remembering your content and trying to engage. By watching it back later, you are able to see you as the audience saw you.

I have lost count of the number of delegates who have said, 'Gosh, I was so nervous, I felt as if I was shaking', only to be shouted down by their peers in the room (and, importantly, supported by the video evidence) that they looked really in command.

Alan – consultant engineer

'I suppose I could say there was a tipping point, it's just I'm not sure when it occurred. I was always nervous before I got up to speak, but after about a year of doing it regularly someone came up afterwards and said, "How come you're so at ease when you're on stage?" It brought me up short and only when I looked back over that period of time did I realize how much more relaxed I really was.'

So, it may look like I'm advocating you just get up there and fake it. Indeed I am. At least for the time being, because confidence is organic, it grows over time, it needs to be nurtured and looked after; it is delicate and easily damaged. However, confidence can be built by doing more and more of the same thing, setting incrementally higher targets for yourself each time.

Think back to when you learned to swim; there was probably a bit of coughing and spluttering to begin with, but at some stage you managed to successfully navigate a width of the pool. When you'd done this several times, you decided you'd attempt a length; your confidence (based on what you had achieved earlier) grew and gave you the impetus to set a more adventurous target.

When I push people on why they feel nervous and unconfident they sometimes reply, 'Well, everyone's looking at me.' The irony is that as they're saying it, everyone is looking at them. Ask a colleague in an informal setting to explain their job role to everyone in the room and it's fine; call it a presentation and it suddenly takes on a disproportionate significance. I know it sounds obvious, but presenting is just talking to other people, it's only by calling it a presentation that it changes how we feel about it.

Part of the problem with confidence is that it's got a bit of a chequered reputation. What I mean by this is that too much confidence can come across as arrogance. It sometimes feels it might be a bit 'showy'. However, it's worth taking the risk and putting it all out there.

It's also the case in a training room environment that people have a real chance to reflect on how their presentation came across and it's very common for them to be able to critique their performance objectively. Often they will say, 'I'd do it differently next time', and it is certainly the case that we get slicker the more we deliver the same content. This is one of the reasons I push home the necessity for rehearsal.

Where confidence sometimes deserts us is if we have to deliver on a subject we're not an expert in. This is quite common in business where the boss might say they want you to present the monthly figures to the management team or some such thing. People seem to get very frightened of being exposed in these situations, as if they're supposed to know everything about a topic.

In the far future, we might aspire to being truly charismatic, but for now concentrate on the next presentation and build your skills as you go. Often we don't even notice the change in our confidence, not until we look back later.

Founding father of Apple, Steve Jobs, tells a fascinating story of how he got to be where he was, which involves all the seemingly unrelated things that interested him in his journey through life, including playing about with font designs and being involved in publishing a magazine, which eventually resulted in him bringing everything together in Apple. Reflecting on this he says, 'You can only join the dots looking back.'

I think the same is true of confidence, one of the cornerstones of the truly accomplished presenter. Confidence can 'get you up there' in the first place, but more than this, it can give you gravitas, the status of 'knowledgeable expert'. It makes audiences feel like they're in 'safe hands' and is an absolute boon when things go wrong, as they inevitably will.

We build confidence, incrementally, in almost imperceptible steps forwards as we travel through life and, as I said, it's only in looking back that we're truly able to see that.

Building block number one is competence. It's hard, though not impossible, to look confident if we don't know what we're talking about, so work hard at the nuts and bolts of your topic and build yourself a bedrock of knowledge to fall back on. If you can look yourself in the mirror and say 'I know my stuff' then it's onwards and upwards from there.

Sporting analogies are rife in business and I'll borrow one now to make my next point; you have to put in the hard yards. Keep practising, keep presenting, pursue every public speaking opportunity you can and learn from each and every one.

Sometimes you have weeks or months to prepare for a formal presentation, say, for example, the annual company conference, but often there's a gap that needs filling with some well-chosen words, a leaving 'do', a thank you speech, a friend's birthday, a media voxpop.

If it's sprung on me, these are the things that will probably go through my head.

What will I say, list of 3, who's listening, read the room, keep it short, start positively, how will I bring it to an impactful conclusion?

Whatever you say, it doesn't have to be perfect. As long as there's some kind of structure to it, you're reasonably coherent and you express how you really feel, you won't go far wrong, and it's just this kind of opportunity which really builds confidence. It's like an algorithm; people who did this, went on to do this!

The very fact that so many people are terrified of public speaking means that you'll win friends and admirers if you're simply prepared to 'have a go'. And the more goes you have a go at, the better you get and the more relaxed you feel.

When it comes to 'charisma', well who wouldn't want to be seen as a charismatic presenter? My advice would be to wait until someone bestows the term upon you. It's not for us to decide if we're charismatic; it's for others. I think of it like a knighthood; someone else decides you warrant it!

Adding value

I talked earlier about the added value you bring to a presentation. What is it that the audience gets by having you there, which they wouldn't understand by simply reading your draft script? Let's take the example of the monthly figures and think it through. There would be little benefit in going through the profit and loss account line by line. Your audience is much more likely to be looking for top line figures and exceptions (perhaps higher than average sales of a particular product line). On this basis your presentation should draw them towards the headlines and the purpose of you being there is to provide some 'commentary' on them. This is where you add value and it's your opinion and insight which counts every bit as much as the figures themselves.

In a live teaching scenario, I purposely let delegates choose the subject matter they want to talk about and encourage them to pick something they feel strongly over. This is partly to get away from the situation described above, where you might be given a topic you're not confident about, but it is mainly because passion is an important part of performance. If we have firm opinions about a subject, we are more likely to articulate them with verve. There are a couple of important points here. The first is to be aware that if you choose a subject which you not only feel passionate about, but is also something highly emotive, you need to be careful to control your passion, it could spill over into a rant.

The second point is to be aware that if you feel strongly, you're more likely to remember your content; it's just a case of structuring things in the right order.

One of the reasons most often cited for lack of confidence or being nervous is that people are worried they'll forget what they were going to say. And yet on dozens of presentation skills courses I have seen delegates spend hours writing and preparing their notes, to glance at them just once or twice. Occasionally they will admonish themselves afterwards for having left out a particular point, but as we outlined in Chapter 17, the audience doesn't know that.

The great benefit of developing confidence over time is that the audience gets to see more of you and your character and it is this unique take on the world which gives you the best chance of engaging with them.

Structure

If, as we've ascertained, our nervous feelings increase and our confidence disappears when we haven't prepared enough, what can we do in circumstances that don't allow for meticulous writing and rehearsal? How can we pull a presentation together quickly?

The answer to this is to have a set structure, so whatever the topic, you can fit it into the template you have built. The outline that I'll discuss here is not the only structure you can use, but it contains the fundamentally important points, which I've seen used successfully by dozens of business people.

When we examined the issue of writing a presentation, we outlined the following basic structure: 1) Tell them what you're going to tell them, 2) Tell them and 3) Tell them what you've told them. This is a good starting point as it sets up a beginning (where you signpost, in brief, the content you're going to present), you go on to deliver that content (in more detail) and then you sum up (in a similarly succinct fashion to the opening) as you bring your presentation to a close.

In Chapter 10 we looked in detail about how to open, so you've got a starting point to your presentation. Managing the audience's expectation through early signposting is important if they're to follow the flow of your address. At this stage it is also usually a good idea to state the purpose of your presentation; for example: 'Today I'm going to talk you through this month's sales figures and draw your attention to the important headlines, so we are better able as a team to draw up a strategy for next month's sales push.' Or the following: 'The reason for my presentation today is to alert you to the dangers of using a mobile phone while driving, so that we can improve road safety.'

If you can't find a simple statement like this to sum up what you're going to say, you probably need to re-think your presentation. There is only so much that can be achieved by a stand-up address and if you think back to the most memorable speech you've heard you can probably only recall a handful of points that were made. The answer is to keep it simple; too often I've seen people try and take on topics that are much too broad, or cover a subject in too much detail.

So far, we've 'told them what we're going to tell them'. How do we go on from here to develop the main body of the presentation? I think the simplicity rule applies again here and I always recommend the development of three key arguments to support your set-up. You can try this now by considering three reasons it's a bad idea to use a mobile phone while driving. There are probably more than three, but what are the most important? If you have a long list of points to support your rationale, can you cluster some together and keep your presentation down to those three key areas?

This process of simplification does two things. First, it shortens your opening statement and doesn't tax the audience's memory too much, and second, you have a much better chance of remembering your content, delivering it in a logical way and maintaining a good flow to your speech.

Persuasion

Many presentations involve an element of persuasion and we can embed a formula for this within our overall structure. Many years ago, when working in advertising, I came across this 'A, B, C' system and have used it on countless occasions since to sense check my 'persuasiveness'.

A, B, C system of persuasion

There are three simple questions that need to be answered before we begin to build a case to persuade.

A Who are we talking to?
We all know the importance of understanding our target audience, otherwise how can we hope to engage them. Finding out as much as you can about them in advance will help you formulate your ideas.

B What do we want them to do?
In advertising circles, this is known as the 'call to action'. What do we want our audience to do as a consequence of listening to us? How do we want them to act differently?

> ### C Why should they do it?
> What is the list of reasons we can give to motivate the people
> in front of us? This part of the formula includes the three
> arguments I outlined earlier.

A final sense check is to ask yourself whether 'C' is a good enough
reason to make 'A' do 'B'. If not, think again. So is that list of arguments compelling enough to motivate this audience into taking the
action I'm recommending?

Even when your presentation isn't about persuasion (it may
simply be a dissemination of information), the three key points
system works well as a structural tool.

Let's take the presentation of the sales figures again and consider the points you may want to make. Example: 'So, today I'd
like to take you through the success from last month, the areas
where we underachieved against target (and the reasons for that)
and point you towards where I think the opportunities are for sales
growth next month.'

The signposting is simple, for both you and the audience, and
you have a clear flow to your story, making it easier to remember.
It can be a good idea to carry on signposting as you deliver your
address. It may sound something like this: 'I've now outlined the
pluses and minuses from last month's sales drive and given you my
reasons for why this is. I'd now like to look forward and use these
figures as a springboard to future sales, by defining the areas I
think we should focus on.'

After you've outlined your third point there are a number of
options on how to finish, which will be dependent on what you're
trying to achieve. Whichever you choose, you first of all have to
sum up what you've talked about and in many cases this will be
pretty much like a repeat of your opening. After that, you may
have a big bang finish (again, see Chapter 11 for further advice on
this). You might decide to throw the debate open to the floor so
that everyone can have their input (either as a formal Q & A or a

facilitated group discussion), or it may be the case that you have a call to action; you want to ask your audience to do something, like sign up for the road safety campaign, for example.

Presenting under pressure

There's a good deal of detail in the description of how to pull a presentation together under pressure and when the heat's on you might not remember it all, so I have outlined a short-form version to act as an aide-memoire. If you keep this in your head, you won't go far wrong.

Short-form presentation structure

1 Opening
State what you intend to do with your presentation, signpost and give the audience a reason to listen (be tough on yourself with your preparation and ask 'what's the point?').

2 Middle
Outline your three main reasons or arguments. If there is going to be a call to action, use the A, B, C formula when you are doing your preparation.

3 Summary
Think through what the point of you being there is and make sure you've answered that question, for yourself, but more importantly for your audience.

Editing

Finally, let's think about the process of editing your presentation. Often our starting point is to think how we're going to spin it out to fill the allotted time, but audiences can sense this: they know if there's a lot of padding.

If you've been given an allocated length, it's true that I advocate coming in bang on time, I think it's part of being a professional, but if the timings are more open ended, make it as long as it needs to be and no more.

To illustrate the point about good editing, I always tell the following story when I'm training in presentation skills.

The duck story

I was watching an episode of the television programme *Countryfile*, which contained an item about an old gentleman who made walking sticks. His sticks were unique because he'd carve the handle into the shape of a duck's head.

To finish the item, the presenter was interviewing the old curmudgeon, who was whittling away at one of his sticks, and said to him, 'It's fascinating the way you do that, could you teach me?' To which the stick man replied, 'Yes, it's easy, you just cut off all the bits that don't look like duck!'

This teaches us a great lesson about relevance. Be tough on yourself when you're editing and keep asking if everything you're saying is adding to the point of your presentation. Cut out all the bits that don't look like duck.

Using a set structure will help you get used to developing presentations that have a logical flow and over time this will bolster your confidence. Add to this good editing skills and you will avoid rambling and keep your audience engaged. The more this happens, the better you will feel when you're on your feet.

Activity

Practise the A, B, C formula of persuasion. Think of something you feel strongly about and then imagine you are trying to convince a person with the opposite view to your way of thinking. Draw up the arguments you would use.

Summary points

- At first you may have to 'fake' confidence, but it will build with practice.
- Presentations are the same as just talking to colleagues; don't build them up to be something scary.
- Think through the 'added value' you bring to a topic; it's your opinion and insight that matters.
- Passion is important, but keep it under control.
- Practise using a set structure; it will help if you have to produce a presentation at short notice.

21
What next?

As far as I can see, you're pretty much ready to take the stage. Whatever your past experience has been of presenting, I hope some of the ideas outlined in this book are of positive benefit. Sometimes the best learning is about simply avoiding the mistakes. I hope you manage that too.

For some food for thought about where to take your presentation skills next, I have put together some notes to suggest a possible way forward.

Beyond best practice

In a previous book that I co-authored with Professor Cary L Cooper called *Business and the Beautiful Game* (published by Kogan Page), we considered what those involved in the commercial sector could learn from examining the world of soccer. Underpinning this idea was the thought that there was something beyond best practice. It seemed that the mantra of the 1990s that urged us to seek out the best in our own industry had its limitations. Chase the leaders and by the time you get to where they are, they will have moved on. Therefore, we theorized that by looking at other aspects of our lives, we might be able to translate some of the lessons learned into our own environment.

The same is true, I believe, of presentation skills, and an arena where we can draw on hard-won experience is live theatre. Given that the best way to improve our presentation skills is to practise, practise, practise, joining a local theatrical society and having the opportunity to appear on stage is a great way to increase your personal 'flying hours'. Perhaps one of the added benefits of this is that it allows the opportunity to try things out behind the mask of the character you are playing. You will also have been given a script, meaning the writing phase has been done for you!

Projection

Acting has its roots far away in the past, before all the technology we now take for granted had been invented. Often this was combined with the task of playing to a large audience, some of whom would inevitably be a long way from the stage. Maybe this is why 'acting' necessitates being 'larger than life'. Gestures are bigger, the voice is used in a grander fashion and facial expressions are more pronounced. How else would the watching public get a sense of what the cast is attempting to portray? Go too far and there is a risk of 'hamming it up', but the mistake that lots of amateur actors and, coincidentally, presenters make is that they fail to 'act up' enough. The stage (whether theatrical or commercial) requires you to be bigger than normal in order to convey your message.

A great way of illustrating this is to watch yourself on video. Do you really look as if you are passionate when you hit the critical bit of your speech? Is your emotion conveyed right to the back of the room? Unless you are a 'natural', it is unlikely. The way we speak needs to be more pronounced. We have to articulate our words more clearly than normal; pauses that might seem like a lifetime when you are standing up there shrink to a mere beat when you reflect back on them.

I am not advocating here that you turn yourself into some kind of a parody of Shakespearean grandeur, or bellow and gesticulate so wildly that you put fear into the first three rows of audience members, but if you 'turn it up' by a notch or two you will be amazed how much more convincing you look and sound.

Tools of the trade

Enhancing the way you look, sound and act are all part of being a great speaker. What we wear becomes part of the representation of what we are seeking to put across. The 'staging' of the event is vitally important. Who is in charge of lighting and sound? If you cannot be heard, or even worse seen, because dimming the lights to enhance the slide show has left you in semi-darkness, it will unsettle your audience.

Character

Mostly the character up there is you, or at least a slightly exaggerated version, which means being true to yourself, so people still recognize you during the post-presentation reception.

Many professional presenters illustrate their stories by 'becoming' the characters in them. A friend of mine in education 'plays out' a conversation between a teacher and a toddler by physically taking up the different positions of each and changing voice from 'authoritative' to 'squeaky'. It's funny, endearing and makes his point in a very powerful way.

These are, of course, extremes and they take practice, skill and a high degree of courage to achieve, but they make the point that 'characterization' is important. It is worth noting here, as I do elsewhere, the bigger the performance, the greater the risk. The truth is that it is much more likely you will look like an idiot if you attempt this kind of thing and don't manage to pull it off. What counterbalances the risk though is if you can deliver well, under such circumstances, people will remember it for a long time to come.

Frequency

Most actors who rehearse for the theatre get multiple chances to deliver their script. Talk to some at the end of a long run and they will tell you how much easier it became as time went by. There is a lesson here about the difference between rehearsal and performance. Just as with sports stars, who might practise on the training ground, it is never the same when you hit the field of play. In front of a live audience, you will find out whether your one-liners are funny or not, you will discover what it is that engages people – and often it will not be the parts you thought – and you will come to understand what they want more of and, critically, what they would like less of. All of this might not mean changing the content, but the way you deliver it, the running order, how your words blend with the visuals or the pauses you take. Just as in acting.

Familiarity

Linked to frequency is the key element of familiarity. The better acquainted you become with a presentation, the more at ease you are in delivering it. No longer are you worried about 'forgetting your lines'; instead you can start to consider the other elements that will add weight to what you are saying. The pace and tone of your delivery, where you place your emphasis, how you use your passion – all these things are important in bringing the words to life.

Actors talk about 'finding the character'. What they mean is that beyond the lines they need to learn there will be traits like an accent, a mannerism, a way of standing and moving around – all the elements that are the 'essence' of who they are playing. None of this can be achieved until they are 100 per cent comfortable with the script, having learned it by heart. I am not advocating you have to be able to deliver your speech verbatim, from a script you have written, but simply saying your ability to 'enhance' the words will be much improved once you are familiar with the content.

If you don't see yourself as a budding actor, you might not share my enthusiasm for theatre as a means of improving presentation skills. However, there are some excellent learning points we can all draw from theatre and you would be amazed at the number of professional presenters who 'trod the boards' at some point in their past life.

And finally...

I hope some of this advice proves to be useful. Even if it just helps to get you up on the stage in the first place then it is mission accomplished, because once you're there, I promise you, you will be able to handle it.

Think back to what I said at the start – this book is called *Develop* **Your** *Presentation Skills*, and in the final analysis, it is all about you – that is who the audience has come to see.

Be yourself, be as well rehearsed as you possibly can and be prepared for the audience to love you. More than anything else though, go out there and enjoy it!

From 4 December 2025 the EU Responsible Person (GPSR) is:
eucomply oÜ, Pärnu mnt. 139b – 14, 11317 Tallinn, Estonia
www.eucompliancepartner.com

www.ingramcontent.com/pod-product-compliance
Lightning Source LLC
Chambersburg PA
CBHW071608210326
41597CB00019B/3457

9 781398 622616